ideals

Ground Meat
COOKBOOK

by Naomi Arbit and June Turner

Ideals Publishing Corp.
Milwaukee, Wisconsin

Introduction

The question of what to make with a pound of hamburger gets some surprisingly delicious answers when best-selling authors Naomi Arbit and June Turner focus their creative attention on the problem. The simplicity of hamburgers is expanded to include new versions of old favorites as well as superb international dishes.

Arbit and Turner have compiled a collection of recipes that illustrate that ground meat, when combined with other tasty ingredients, results in delicious casseroles, soups, sandwiches, and crepes. And a ground meat staple—the meat loaf—is spotlighted in an assortment of mouth-watering recipes that will take the meat loaf to center stage on your dining table.

The versatility of ground meat is an unparalleled advantage for today's cooks. Those who are preparing meals on a small budget will be delighted to discover that many of the dishes use only a single pound of ground meat, yet serve six or more people.

Watch for the smiles when tonight's dinner features one of the delicious recipes from the *Ground Meat Cookbook* and stand back to accept the compliments.

Cover recipe:
Sweet-Sour Pork Patties,
page 52

ISBN 0-8249-3005-3

Copyright © MCMLXXXI by Naomi Arbit and June Turner

All rights reserved.
Printed and bound in the United States of America.
Published by Ideals Publishing Corporation.
11315 Watertown Plank Road
Milwaukee, WI 53226
Published simultaneously in Canada.

Cookbook Editor
Julie Hogan

Food Stylist
Susan Noland

Contents

Appetizers and Patés

Meatballs Madras

Makes 50 meatballs.

- 1½ pounds ground beef or combination of beef, veal, and pork
- 2 eggs, lightly beaten
- 1 cup mixed dried fruits, such as apricots, prunes, raisins, or apples, snipped into bits
- ½ cup minced onion
- ½ cup fresh bread crumbs
- 1 teaspoon salt
  Dash Tabasco sauce
- 2 tablespoons vegetable oil or margarine
- 1 cup sweet vermouth

Combine all ingredients, except oil and vermouth, in a mixing bowl; mix gently. Shape into 50 1-inch meatballs. Heat oil in a large frying pan. Sauté several meatballs at a time, turning to brown evenly. Place in a heated chafing dish. Heat vermouth until warm. Pour vermouth over meatballs.

Lo-Cal Swedish Meatballs

Makes 48 meatballs.

- 1 pound ground beef
- 1 pound ground veal
- 1 tablespoon dried onion flakes
- 1 thin slice dry white bread, crumbled
- ½ cup skim milk
- 2 teaspoons salt
- ¼ teaspoon black pepper
- ⅛ teaspoon cloves
- ⅛ teaspoon nutmeg

Combine all ingredients; mix thoroughly. Using wet hands, shape mixture into ¾-inch balls. Place on a rack in a flat pan. Bake at 350° for 20 minutes or until brown. Prepare Sauce. Add meatballs to Sauce. Simmer uncovered 10 minutes. Serve in Sauce.

Sauce

- 1 beef bouillon cube
- 1 cup water
- 1 tablespoon dried onion flakes
- 1 cup chopped celery
- 1 cup tomato juice
- ¼ cup lemon juice
- 2 tablespoons Worcestershire sauce
- 2 tablespoons cider vinegar
- 1 tablespoon prepared mustard
- ½ teaspoon salt
- 2 teaspoons sugar or sugar substitute

Combine all ingredients in a saucepan. Cook 20 minutes or until celery is tender; stir occasionally.

Swedish Meatballs

Makes 60 to 80 meatballs.

- 1 pound ground beef, or combination beef, veal, and pork
- ½ cup fine dry bread crumbs
- 1 cup milk, divided
- 1 egg, lightly beaten
- 1½ teaspoons salt, divided
- ½ teaspoon nutmeg
  Dash black pepper
- 2 tablespoons Worcestershire sauce
- 2 tablespoons vegetable oil
- 3 tablespoons flour
- 1 pint light cream

Combine beef, bread crumbs, ½ cup of the milk, egg, 1 teaspoon of the salt, nutmeg, pepper, and Worcestershire sauce; mix thoroughly. Shape into 1-inch balls. Heat the oil in a frying pan. Brown half of the meatballs. Remove from pan and set aside. Brown remaining meatballs. Combine flour and remaining ½ teaspoon salt with pan drippings; blend thoroughly. Slowly blend in cream and remaining ½ cup milk; stir until mixture thickens and comes to a boil. Return meatballs to pan. Heat through.

Turkish Meatballs with Yogurt

Makes 60 to 80 meatballs.

- 1 cup plain yogurt
  Snipped parsley
- 1 tablespoon mint flakes
- ¼ teaspoon salt
- 4 thin slices white bread, crusts trimmed, torn into 1-inch pieces
- ⅓ cup water
- 2 pounds ground lamb
- ¼ cup minced onion
- ½ teaspoon salt
- ¼ teaspoon ground cumin
- ¼ teaspoon black pepper
- ¼ cup flour
  Vegetable oil

Combine yogurt, parsley, mint, and salt; blend thoroughly. Refrigerate until serving time. Soak bread in water until water is nearly absorbed. Squeeze out excess water. Combine bread with all ingredients, except flour and oil; mix well. Shape rounded teaspoons of mixture into balls. Roll each ball in flour. Heat 1-inch oil in a frying pan. Fry meatballs until golden. Drain on paper toweling. (If necessary, meatballs may be reheated in a 350° oven.) Serve meatballs on toothpicks around a bowl of the prepared yogurt.

Tamale Tidbits

Makes 90 meatballs.

    2 cups crumbled corn bread
    ½ cup enchilada sauce
    1½ pounds ground beef
    1 clove garlic, crushed
    1 teaspoon ground cumin
    1 teaspoon chili powder
    1 teaspoon salt

Combine all ingredients; mix well. Shape into 90 1-inch balls. Bake uncovered at 350° for 20 to 30 minutes, until brown. While meatballs are baking, prepare Sauce. Place meatballs in a chafing dish. Pour Sauce over meatballs. Serve with toothpicks.

Sauce

    1 8-ounce can tomato sauce
    ½ cup enchilada sauce
    1 cup grated Monterey Jack cheese

Combine all ingredients. Heat until cheese melts and sauce is bubbly hot.

Beef and Sausage Rounds

Makes 60.

    1 pound bulk pork sausage
    1 pound ground beef
    1 pound process American cheese, cut in cubes
    1 teaspoon crushed oregano
    1 tablespoon Worcestershire sauce
    1 tablespoon minced onion or dried onion flakes
    2 loaves party rye bread

Sauté pork until no longer pink. Add beef and sauté until brown; drain fat. Add cheese; stir until melted. Add seasonings; blend well. Spread on rye bread slices*. Place on a baking sheet. Bake at 350° for 8 to 10 minutes. Add another 5 minutes, if frozen.

*May be made ahead to this point and frozen. Add 5 minutes to baking time.

Chicken or Turkey Soufflés

Makes 2¾ cups.

    2 cups minced or ground cooked chicken or turkey
    1 3-ounce package cream cheese, softened
    ½ cup mayonnaise
    1 tablespoon lemon juice
    1 tablespoon capers
      Dash Tabasco sauce

Combine all ingredients; mix thoroughly. Mound onto toast rounds. Broil until puffy.

Steak Tartare

Makes 4 to 6 servings.

    1 pound ground round or sirloin
    1 egg
    1 teaspoon salt
    1 teaspoon freshly ground black pepper
    1 clove garlic, minced
    1 tablespoon Worcestershire sauce
    1 teaspoon Tabasco sauce
    1 tablespoon snipped parsley
    ¼ cup minced onion

Combine all ingredients in a bowl; mix lightly. Mound on a bed of shredded lettuce. Arrange party rye slices around edges.

Stuffed Mushrooms

Makes 24.

    1 pound pork sausage, cooked and drained
    ½ cup dry bread crumbs
    1 egg, lightly beaten
    24 large mushroom caps, wiped clean with a damp cloth

Combine sausage, bread crumbs, and egg; mix thoroughly. Fill mushroom caps. Place on a buttered broiler pan. Broil about 6 inches from heat source for 8 to 10 minutes until sizzling.

Chicken Salad Spread

Makes 2½ cups.

    2 cups minced or ground, cooked chicken
    ¼ cup minced celery
    ½ cup mayonnaise
    2 tablespoons sour cream
    1 tablespoon sherry
    1 tablespoon lemon juice
      Sliced ripe olives
      Paprika

Combine all ingredients, except sliced olives and paprika; mix well. Garnish with olives and sprinkle on paprika. Serve with toast or crackers.

Deviled Ham Spread

Makes 3¼ cups.

    2 cups ground, cooked ham
    2 hard-cooked eggs, minced
    ½ small onion, minced
    1 tablespoon minced sweet pickle
    ½ cup mayonnaise
    1 tablespoon Worcestershire sauce
    2 to 3 drops Tabasco sauce

Combine all ingredients; mix well. Serve with crackers or party rye slices.

Chicken Liver Paté I

Makes 4 to 6 servings.

  2 tablespoons butter
  1 small onion, minced
  1 cup minced mushrooms
  2 tablespoons flour
  ½ cup milk
  1 tablespoon butter
  ½ pound chicken livers, rinsed and dried
  ¼ pound ground round steak
  1 egg
  ½ teaspoon salt
  1 tablespoon brandy
  2 tablespoons sweet vermouth
  2 hard-cooked eggs, minced
  10 to 12 black olives, minced
  ¼ cup snipped parsley

Melt the 2 tablespoons butter in a frying pan. Add onion and mushrooms and sauté until tender. Sprinkle flour into pan. While stirring, slowly add milk and stir until thickened. Remove from heat and set aside.

Melt the 1 tablespoon butter in a frying pan. Sauté chicken livers until no longer pink. Place livers, ground round, raw egg, salt, brandy, and vermouth in a blender container. Whirl until smooth.

Combine onion-mushroom mixture, meat-liver mixture, hard-cooked eggs, and olives in a mixing bowl. Blend thoroughly.

Spoon into an oiled loaf pan. Cover with foil. Place in a shallow pan filled with 1 inch water. Bake at 350° for 45 minutes. Remove foil and bake for 1 hour.

Refrigerate for 4 to 6 hours before serving. Garnish with parsley. Serve with rye or pumpernickel bread.

Liver Paté

Makes 12 to 14 servings.

  1 pound calves' liver or chicken livers
  2 small onions, sliced
  2 tablespoons chicken fat or butter
  3 hard-cooked eggs
  4 tablespoons chicken fat or butter, softened
  1 teaspoon salt
  ¼ teaspoon black pepper
  1 tablespoon mayonnaise, optional

Gently sauté livers and onions in the 2 table-spoons chicken fat until liver is no longer pink. Remove livers and onions from pan; set aside to cool. Grind livers, onions, and eggs together. Add the 4 tablespoons fat, salt, pepper, and mayonnaise; mix thoroughly. Spoon into a bowl or mold and chill until set. Turn out onto a platter. Serve with sliced cocktail rye bread or crackers or mounded on individual lettuce leaves as a first course.

Chicken Liver Paté II

Makes 4 cups.

  3 tablespoons butter or margarine
  1 pound chicken livers
  ½ pound mushrooms, chopped
  1 tablespoon minced onion
  1 cup sour half-and-half
  1 teaspoon Worcestershire sauce
  1 teaspoon prepared mustard
  2 tablespoons brandy
    Dash red pepper
    Minced parsley
    Melba toast

Melt butter in a small frying pan. Sauté chicken livers until no longer pink. Remove from pan; grind. Add mushrooms and onion to pan; sauté until onion is tender. Remove from pan; cool. Combine ground livers, mushrooms, onion, sour half-and-half, and seasonings; mix well. Spoon into a serving dish. Garnish with parsley. Serve with melba toast.

Ham Spread

Makes 1⅓ cups.

  1 cup ground cooked ham
  ¼ cup finely grated Cheddar cheese
  1 teaspoon prepared mustard
  2 teaspoons pickle relish
  3 tablespoons mayonnaise

Combine all ingredients; mix well. Serve on crackers or party rye slices.

Zippy Ham Spread

Makes 3¼ cups.

  2 cups ground cooked ham
  2 tablespoons prepared mustard
  2 tablespoons horseradish
  1 cup sour cream

Combine all ingredients; blend thoroughly. Serve with rye or pumpernickel bread.

Swedish Meatballs, 4
Chicken Liver Paté, above

Beef

Chuck Chop Suey

Makes 4 to 6 servings.

1 pound ground chuck or ground beef
2 onions, sliced
½ cup sliced mushrooms
8 to 10 water chestnuts, sliced
1 cup canned bean sprouts, drained
3 tablespoons soy sauce
1 teaspoon ginger
1 teaspoon sugar
1 cup beef bouillon
1 tablespoon cornstarch

Sauté beef, onions, and mushrooms in a frying pan for 8 to 10 minutes. Stir in water chestnuts, bean sprouts, soy sauce, ginger, and sugar. Combine bouillon and cornstarch; blend thoroughly. Stir into meat and vegetables. Bring to a boil, stirring until thick and clear. Serve over rice.

Chili I

Makes 4 to 6 servings.

1 pound ground beef
2 to 3 teaspoons chili powder
1 teaspoon sugar
1 rib celery, chopped
1 small onion, chopped
½ green pepper, chopped
1 15-ounce can tomato sauce with tomato bits
½ cup water
1 clove garlic, minced
1 15-ounce can red beans
  Grated Parmesan cheese

Brown meat in a frying pan; drain fat. Add chili powder, sugar, celery, onion, and green pepper; sauté until vegetables are tender. Add tomato sauce, water, and garlic; cover and simmer for 30 minutes. Add beans. Simmer uncovered for 20 minutes. Sprinkle on cheese before serving.

Chili II

Makes 6 servings.

1 pound ground beef
1 onion, chopped
1 rib celery, chopped
½ green pepper, chopped
1 16-ounce can tomatoes, cut up
1 10-ounce package frozen whole kernel corn
1 8-ounce can tomato sauce
1 package chili seasoning mix
2 ounces American cheese, shredded

Brown beef, onion, celery, and green pepper; drain fat. Add remaining ingredients, except cheese. Cover and simmer for 20 minutes, stirring occasionally. Sprinkle on cheese. Cover and heat until cheese begins to melt.

Chili-Mac

Makes 10 servings.

2 pounds ground beef
2 cups chopped onions
2 cloves garlic, minced
1 16-ounce can tomatoes
1 quart tomato juice
2 teaspoons salt
½ green pepper, chopped
2 tablespoons chili powder
½ teaspoon each: cumin, oregano, black pepper
1 bay leaf
1 15-ounce can red kidney beans, drained
½ cup chopped sweet pickles or relish
8 ounces elbow macaroni, prepared according to package directions and drained

Brown beef, onions, and garlic in a large frying pan; drain fat. Add tomatoes, tomato juice, and seasonings. Cover and simmer for 45 minutes. Stir in kidney beans and pickles. Simmer 30 minutes. Remove bay leaf. Add macaroni and stir to mix.

Vegetable Meat Soup

Makes 6 servings.

6 beef bouillon cubes
5 cups boiling water
1 16-ounce can tomatoes
1 onion, chopped
¾ cup chopped celery
1 bay leaf
½ teaspoon salt
  Dash black pepper
½ pound ground beef
1 10-ounce package frozen mixed vegetables
1 teaspoon dried dillweed or ½ teaspoon thyme

Dissolve bouillon in boiling water. Add tomatoes, onion, celery, bay leaf, salt, and pepper. Cover and simmer for 15 minutes. In a small frying pan, sauté beef until just brown; drain fat. Add meat, vegetables, and dill to soup. Simmer until vegetables are tender-crisp. Remove bay leaf and serve.

Meatball Soup

Makes 6 servings.

 6 cups water
 2 beef bones
 2 onions, sliced
 2 carrots, sliced
 1 cup sliced celery
 1 tomato, chopped
 2 cups sauerkraut juice
 2 tablespoons snipped parsley
 1 teaspoon dillweed
 1 teaspoon salt
 ¼ teaspoon black pepper

Combine water, bones, onions, carrots, celery, and tomato in a soup kettle; bring to a boil. Reduce heat to medium; cover and simmer for 1 hour. Strain and return to kettle. Add sauerkraut juice, parsley, dillweed, salt, and pepper. Bring to a boil; reduce heat to medium and simmer while preparing the Meatballs.

Meatballs

 1 pound ground beef
 ½ cup dry bread crumbs
 1 egg, lightly beaten
 ½ teaspoon salt
 ¼ teaspoon black pepper

Combine all ingredients; mix thoroughly. Shape into ½-inch balls. Add to soup and cook over medium heat for 10 minutes.

Dilly Stew

Makes 6 to 8 servings.

 1½ pounds ground beef
 ½ head cabbage, cored and shredded
 2 carrots, cut into chunks
 1 rib celery, cut into chunks
 1 onion, diced
 1 teaspoon salt
 ¼ teaspoon black pepper
 1 teaspoon paprika
 1 teaspoon dillweed
 1 8-ounce can tomato sauce
 1 cup sour half and half
  Cooked noodles

Brown beef; drain fat. Add remaining ingredients, except sour half-and-half and noodles. Simmer for ½ hour. Just before serving, stir in sour half-and-half. Serve over noodles.

Stuffed Hamburgers

Makes 4 servings.

 1½ to 2 pounds ground beef
  Salt and freshly ground pepper to taste
  Blue Cheese, Onion or Ham and Cheese Stuffing

Season ground beef with salt and pepper. Pat into a 12 x 6-inch rectangle on a sheet of waxed paper. Cut into 8 squares with a wet knife. Spread stuffing on 4 squares, leaving a ¼-inch border on all edges. Cover with remaining squares. Press edges together with moistened fingers. Round out corners to seal in filling. Fry or broil to desired doneness. Turn once.

Blue Cheese Stuffing

 ½ cup crumbled blue cheese
 2 tablespoons cream or mayonnaise
 1 tablespoon minced onion

Combine all ingredients; blend thoroughly.

Onion Stuffing

 2 cups minced onion (use only 1 cup onion, if adding bacon)
 2 tablespoons butter or vegetable oil
 ⅛ teaspoon nutmeg
 2 tablespoons sour cream
 ½ cup crumbled, cooked bacon, optional

Sauté onions in butter. Stir in nutmeg, sour cream, and bacon.

Ham and Cheese Stuffing

 4 slices ham
 4 slices Muenster, Swiss or Cheddar cheese

Place ham and cheese on 4 squares of the beef, leaving a ¼-inch border on all edges. Top with remaining squares. Crimp and round off edges.

Burgundy Burgers

Makes 4 servings.

 1 pound ground beef
 ½ cup cracker crumbs
 ¼ cup Burgundy wine
 1 tablespoon chili sauce
 1 teaspoon Worcestershire sauce
 ½ small onion, minced
 ½ teaspoon salt
  Dash black pepper
 4 sesame hamburger rolls, split and toasted

Combine all ingredients, except rolls; mix well. Shape into 4 patties. Broil or grill as desired. Serve on toasted rolls.

Broiled Tournedos

Makes 4 servings.

1½ pounds lean ground beef
¼ cup minced onion
 1 clove garlic, minced
 1 tablespoon Worcestershire sauce
 8 slices bacon

Combine beef, onion, garlic, and Worcestershire sauce; mix well. Shape into 4 patties. Place on a baking sheet. Place in freezer for 30 minutes. Remove patties from freezer. Loosely wrap 1 slice of bacon half way around sides of pattie; wrap second slice of bacon around remaining half of pattie, overlapping ends about ½ inch. Secure bacon with a toothpick at the middle of each overlap. Repeat for each pattie. Broil 5 inches from heat until browned, about 10 minutes. Turn and broil second side. Serve with Mustard Sauce.

Mustard Sauce

½ cup mayonnaise
 2 tablespoons prepared mustard
¼ teaspoon tarragon
 1 teaspoon horseradish

Combine all ingredients in a saucepan. Cook and stir over low heat until warm.

Keep hot grease from splattering by sprinkling a little salt in the pan first.

German Beef Steak

Makes 6 servings.

 2 pounds ground beef, or equal parts beef, veal, and pork
 1 onion, minced
 2 tablespoons snipped parsley
 2 eggs, lightly beaten
   Salt and freshly ground pepper to taste
   Pinch nutmeg
 2 tablespoons flour
 2 tablespoons butter
 2 tablespoons vegetable oil
 2 large onions, sliced and separated into rings
 2 tablespoons dry red wine

Combine beef, onion, parsley, eggs, salt, pepper, nutmeg, and flour; mix gently. Shape into 6 oval patties. Heat butter and oil in a frying pan. Brown hamburgers on 1 side; turn and cook until desired doneness. Place on a heated platter. Sauté onion rings in pan juices until soft and golden. Place on top of burgers. Add wine to pan; bring to a boil, stirring frequently. Pour over hamburgers.

Salisbury Steak

Makes 6 servings.

1½ pounds ground beef
1½ cups fresh bread crumbs
¼ teaspoon salt
¼ teaspoon black pepper
 4 onions, thinly sliced
 2 tablespoons butter or margarine
 1 tablespoon vegetable oil
 2 tablespoons cornstarch
 2 beef bouillon cubes
 1 teaspoon Worcestershire sauce
1½ cups hot water

Combine beef, bread crumbs, salt, and pepper; mix thoroughly. Shape into 6 oval patties. Place on broiler rack.

Sauté onions in butter and oil until tender. Stir in cornstarch, bouillon, Worcestershire sauce, and hot water. Cook and stir constantly until mixture is thickened. Reduce heat to low. Cover and simmer for 10 minutes. Broil hamburgers about 8 minutes on each side, or until desired doneness. Place patties on a warm platter. Pour onion sauce over all.

Taco Casserole

Makes 6 servings.

 1 pound ground beef or combination veal and pork
½ cup chopped onion
 1 clove garlic, minced
½ teaspoon salt
¼ teaspoon black pepper
 1 10-ounce can enchilada sauce
 1 8-ounce can tomato sauce
1½ teaspoons instant coffee crystals
12 corn tortillas*
½ cup water
1½ cups shredded sharp Cheddar cheese
 4 green onions, snipped

Sauté beef, onion, garlic, salt, and pepper until meat is browned; drain fat. Combine sauces and coffee crystals. Mix half of the sauce with the meat. Place ¼ cup of the meat mixture in the center of each tortilla; fold in half. Place open-side up in a 12 x 7½ x 2-inch baking dish. Add water to remaining sauce and pour over tortillas. Sprinkle 1 cup of the cheese over all. Cover with a greased sheet of aluminum foil. Bake at 375° for 25 minutes. Uncover; sprinkle on remaining ½ cup cheese. Bake 2 minutes.

Note: If using frozen tortillas, wrap them in double strength aluminum foil and heat at 375° for 5 minutes or until they separate easily.

Florentine Hamburgers

Makes 8 servings.

 2 pounds ground beef
 1 clove garlic, minced
 1 teaspoon salt
 ½ teaspoon black pepper
 1 egg, beaten
 ½ cup cottage cheese
 ½ 10-ounce package frozen spinach, thawed and
    squeezed dry
 ¼ cup grated Parmesan cheese

Combine ground beef, garlic, salt, and pepper; mix thoroughly. Form into 8 patties. Combine remaining ingredients; mix well. Place 2 tablespoons of the mixture on one half of each pattie. Fold over and seal. Bake at 425° for 20 minutes or until browned.

Tacos

Makes 12 tacos.

 1 pound ground beef
 1 cup chopped onion
 ½ cup chopped green pepper
 1 clove garlic, crushed
 1 8-ounce can tomato sauce
 1 tablespoon chili powder
 1 teaspoon ground cumin
    Dash Tabasco sauce
 12 taco shells
 3 tomatoes, chopped
 ½ medium head lettuce, shredded
 ½ pound Cheddar cheese, grated

Sauté beef, onion, green pepper, and garlic until beef is no longer red. Drain excess fat. Add tomato sauce and seasonings. Simmer for 20 minutes or until somewhat thickened, stirring often. Warm taco shells in a 350° oven for 5 minutes. Spoon beef mixture into shells. Top with tomatoes, lettuce, and cheese.

Barbecued Beef

Makes 8 servings.

 2 pounds ground beef
 1 onion, minced
 1 clove garlic, crushed
 2 tablespoons vinegar
 3 tablespoons brown sugar
 2 tablespoons lemon juice
 1 cup catsup
 2 tablespoons Worcestershire sauce
 ½ teaspoon dry mustard
 1 teaspoon salt
 8 hamburger rolls, split and toasted

Brown beef, onion, and garlic in a large frying pan; drain fat. Stir in remaining ingredients. Simmer for 10 to 15 minutes. Spoon onto rolls.

Deviled Beef Sandwiches

Makes 4 servings.

 1 pound ground beef
 ⅓ cup chili sauce
 1½ teaspoons prepared mustard
 1½ teaspoons horseradish
 1 tablespoon minced onion
 1½ teaspoons Worcestershire sauce
 ½ teaspoon salt
 ¼ teaspoon black pepper
 4 hamburger rolls, split

Combine all ingredients, except rolls; blend thoroughly. Spread on cut sides of rolls. Place on a broiler rack about 2 inches below heat source. Broil as desired.

Broiled Beef Sandwiches

Makes 4 servings.

 ¾ pound ground beef
 ¼ pound Cheddar cheese, grated
 1 tablespoon minced onion
 1 tablespoon catsup
 1 teaspoon prepared mustard
 ¼ teaspoon salt
 4 slices bread, toasted on 1 side

Combine all ingredients, except bread; blend thoroughly. Spread on untoasted side of bread all the way to the edges. Cut each slice diagonally in half. Place on broiler rack. Broil 6 to 10 minutes or as desired.

Speedy Bean 'n' Bacon Joes

Makes 6 servings.

 1 onion, minced
 ½ green pepper, minced
 1 tablespoon butter or margarine
 1 pound ground beef
 1 10¾-ounce can condensed bean with bacon soup
 ½ cup water
 ⅓ cup catsup
 6 hamburger buns, split and toasted

Sauté onion and green pepper in butter until tender. Add beef and brown, stirring to break up meat; drain fat. Add soup, water, and catsup. Simmer 5 minutes, stirring constantly. Add more water, if desired. Serve on buns.

Barbecue Squares

Makes 4 to 6 servings.

10 refrigerated flaky biscuits
1 pound ground beef
½ onion, chopped
1 rib celery, chopped
½ cup barbecue sauce
4 ounces Cheddar cheese, grated

Separate biscuits; press into an ungreased 9 x 13-inch pan. Cover bottom and 1 inch up the sides to form a crust. Brown ground beef, onion, and celery; drain. Stir in barbecue sauce; simmer for 3 to 4 minutes. Spread hot meat mixture over crust. Sprinkle on cheese. Bake in a preheated 375° oven for 15 minutes. Cut and serve.

Chuck Steaks with Sauce

Makes 4 to 6 servings.

½ cup butter or margarine
1 clove garlic, crushed
1 onion, chopped
½ pound mushrooms, sliced
  Pinch thyme
¼ cup bottled steak sauce
¼ cup Burgundy wine
1½ pounds ground chuck, formed into
  4 to 6 oval patties

Melt butter in a frying pan. Sauté garlic, onion, and mushrooms until tender. Add remaining ingredients, except meat. Simmer for about 10 minutes. While sauce is simmering, broil patties as desired. Ladle sauce over patties.

Pizza Loaf

Makes 8 to 10 servings.

1 pound ground beef
½ cup chopped onion
1 6-ounce can tomato paste
1 tablespoon Worcestershire sauce
½ teaspoon oregano
1 loaf Italian bread, cut in half lengthwise
¼ cup butter or margarine, softened
1½ cups shredded mozzarella cheese

Brown beef and onion in a frying pan; drain. Stir in tomato paste, Worcestershire sauce, and oregano. Place bread cut-side up on a large baking sheet. Spread with butter; toast under broiler until golden. Spread meat mixture on tops. Sprinkle on cheese. Broil 4 to 5 minutes or until cheese is slightly melted. Slice and serve.

Chopped Steak Diane

Makes 4 servings.

1 pound lean ground beef
½ teaspoon salt
⅛ teaspoon black pepper
3 tablespoons butter or margarine
¼ cup minced onion
1 teaspoon Dijon-style mustard
1 teaspoon Worcestershire sauce
2 tablespoons snipped parsley
½ cup dry vermouth
¼ cup brandy

Combine beef, salt, and pepper; mix thoroughly. Shape into 4 ½-inch thick patties. Brown quickly on both sides in 2 tablespoons of the butter. Remove from pan and keep warm. Add remaining 1 tablespoon butter, onion, mustard, Worcestershire sauce, and parsley to pan; bring to a boil. Stir in vermouth; simmer for 2 to 3 minutes. Heat brandy in a small saucepan but do not boil. Return patties to frying pan. Pour brandy over patties; flame for 30 seconds. Serve with a sprig of parsley.

Sauerbraten Burgers

Makes 6 servings.

¾ cup crushed gingersnap cookies
1 8-ounce can tomato sauce
½ cup minced onion
1 clove garlic, minced
½ teaspoon salt
  Dash black pepper
1½ pounds ground beef
¼ cup water
2 tablespoons brown sugar
3 tablespoons vinegar
1 teaspoon prepared mustard

Combine ½ cup of the gingersnaps, ¼ cup of the tomato sauce, onion, garlic, salt, pepper, and beef; mix well. Shape into 6 patties. Brown burgers in a frying pan; drain excess fat. Combine remaining tomato sauce, water, brown sugar, vinegar, and mustard. Pour over burgers. Cover and simmer 10 to 15 minutes. Place burgers on a warm serving platter. Stir remaining gingersnaps into sauce in pan; cook until thickened and bubbly. Pass sauce to pour over burgers.

Beef Noodle Stroganoff

Makes 6 servings.

- 1 pound ground beef
- ½ onion, chopped
- 1 clove garlic, minced
- 1 4-ounce can sliced mushrooms, drained, reserve juice
- 1 10¾-ounce can condensed beef broth
- 1 tablespoon lemon juice
- ¼ teaspoon black pepper
- 4 ounces medium noodles
- 1 cup sour cream
- 2 tablespoons snipped parsley

Brown beef, onion, and garlic in a frying pan; drain fat. Add mushroom juice, beef broth, lemon juice, and pepper to pan. Stir in uncooked noodles. Cover and simmer 15 minutes or until noodles are tender. Stir in mushrooms and sour cream. Heat through, but do not boil. Sprinkle on parsley and serve.

Hamburger Stroganoff

Makes 4 to 6 servings.

- 1 pound ground beef
- 3 slices bacon, diced
- ½ cup chopped onion
  Dash Tabasco sauce
- 1 10¾-ounce can cream of mushroom soup
- 1 cup plain yogurt

Brown beef and bacon in a frying pan. Add onion and cook until tender; drain fat. Stir in Tabasco and soup. Cook over low heat for 15 minutes, stirring often. Stir in yogurt and heat through, without boiling. Serve with hot, fluffy rice.

Shepherd's Pie

Makes 6 servings.

- 2 onions, minced
- 1 clove garlic, minced
- 2 tablespoons butter or margarine
- 1 pound ground beef
- 1 teaspoon instant beef bouillon granules
- ½ cup hot water
- 1 tablespoon catsup
- 1 teaspoon Worcestershire sauce
- ½ teaspoon mustard
- ¼ cup warm milk
- 3 tablespoons butter or margarine
- 1 teaspoon salt
- ¼ teaspoon black pepper
- 3 cups mashed potatoes (4 to 6 potatoes)

Sauté onions and garlic in butter until tender. Add beef and sauté until brown; drain. Stir in beef granules, water, catsup, Worcestershire sauce, and mustard. Pour into a lightly buttered, 9-inch square baking dish. Add warm milk, butter, salt, and pepper to mashed potatoes; beat until light and fluffy. Spread over the meat mixture to edges of the dish. Run a fork over the top for a rippled effect. Bake at 425° for 30 minutes or until potatoes are golden brown. Cut into squares.

Broiled Ground Beef Triangles

Makes 8 to 10 triangles.

- 4 to 5 slices of bread, toasted on 1 side
  Softened butter
  Prepared mustard
- ½ pound ground beef
- 1 teaspoon prepared horseradish
- 1 tablespoon milk
- ½ teaspoon salt
- ½ teaspoon black pepper
- 1 tablespoon instant minced onion

Spread untoasted side of bread with butter and mustard. Combine remaining ingredients; mix lightly. Spread on top of mustard to the edges of the bread. Broil meat-side up 5 to 7 minutes, or until desired doneness. Cut each sandwich into 2 triangles.

Frosted Hamburgers

Makes 4 servings.

- 2 slices bacon, cooked, drained, and crumbled
- 1 small onion, minced
- 1 pound ground beef
- 1 egg, lightly beaten
- ⅓ cup mayonnaise
- 1 teaspoon Worcestershire sauce
- ½ teaspoon dry mustard
- 1 small zucchini, thinly sliced
- 4 thick tomato slices
- 2 tablespoons grated Parmesan cheese
- 4 hamburger rolls, split and toasted

Combine bacon, onion, ground beef, and egg; mix well. Shape into 4 patties. Mix mayonnaise, Worcestershire sauce, and mustard together. Broil patties on 1 side for 3 minutes; turn and broil for 3 minutes. Top with zucchini, tomato, a dollop of mayonnaise sauce, and a sprinkle of Parmesan cheese. Broil for 3 to 4 minutes until puffy and bubbly. Serve on toasted hamburger rolls.

Beef Stroganoff

Makes 4 servings.

- 1 pound ground beef
- 1 medium onion, chopped
- 1 clove garlic, minced
- ½ teaspoon dry mustard
- ½ cup beef bouillon
- ½ cup mayonnaise
- ½ cup sour cream
- 1 4-ounce can sliced mushrooms, drained

Sauté beef, onion, and garlic until beef is browned and onion is tender; drain fat. Stir in remaining ingredients; cook over very low heat for 15 minutes or until heated through. Do not boil. Serve over rice or noodles.

Mexicali Casserole

Makes 6 to 8 servings.

- ½ pound ground beef
- 4 15½-ounce cans chili con carne with beans
- 4 green onions, sliced
- 10 to 12 pitted ripe olives, cut in half
- ½ green pepper, chopped
- 4 tomatoes, sliced
- ¾ cup grated Cheddar cheese

Brown beef in a frying pan; drain. In a 3-quart casserole, layer beef, chili, onion, olives, green pepper, tomatoes, and cheese, ending with cheese. Bake at 375° for 30 to 35 minutes, until hot and bubbly.

Dilled Stroganoff

Makes 6 servings.

- 1 pound ground beef
- 1 medium onion, chopped
- 8 ounces fresh mushrooms, sliced
- 1 clove garlic, minced
- ½ teaspoon dried dillweed
- ¾ cup beef broth
- ½ cup dry red wine
- ¼ cup catsup
- 1 tablespoon flour
- 1 cup sour cream
- Snipped parsley

Brown beef, onion, mushrooms, and garlic in a frying pan; drain fat. Stir in dillweed, beef broth, wine, and catsup. Cover and simmer for 10 minutes. Stir flour into sour cream. Stir sour cream into beef mixture. Cook and stir until thick and bubbly. Serve on a platter of hot buttered noodles garnished with snipped parsley.

Beef and Potato Casserole

Makes 6 servings.

- 1 pound ground beef
- 1 onion, chopped
- 1 clove garlic, minced
- 2 carrots, cut into strips
- 1 6-ounce can tomato paste
- 2 cups beef bouillon
- ½ teaspoon salt
- ¼ teaspoon black pepper
- ½ bay leaf
- ½ teaspoon thyme
- 1 20-ounce package frozen hash brown potatoes

Sauté beef, onion, garlic, and carrots for 10 minutes; drain. Add tomato paste, bouillon, and seasonings. Simmer for 10 minutes. Place potatoes in a greased 9 x 13-inch baking dish. Top with meat mixture. Cover and bake at 350° for 1 hour or until potatoes are tender.

Mock Lobster Sauce

Makes 4 servings.

- 1 pound ground beef
- 2 beef bouillon cubes
- 1 cup boiling water
- 4 cloves garlic, minced
- 1 teaspoon Chinese brown gravy sauce
- 1 teaspoon soy sauce
- 4 teaspoons sugar
- 3 eggs, beaten
- 2 teaspoons cornstarch

Brown meat in a frying pan. Drain fat. Dissolve bouillon in water. Add bouillon, garlic, gravy sauce, soy sauce, and sugar. Pour eggs evenly over top. Let set slightly. Stir into meat. Stir in cornstarch and cook until thickened. Serve with rice.

Quick Tacos

Makes 12 servings.

- 1 pound ground beef, browned and drained
- 1 small can taco sauce
- 1 tablespoon chili powder
- 12 taco shells
- 1 medium onion, chopped
- 2 tomatoes, chopped
- ½ head lettuce, shredded
- ½ pound Cheddar cheese, grated

Combine first 3 ingredients in a saucepan. Simmer 5 to 6 minutes. Fill taco shells with meat. Serve with bowls of remaining ingredients.

Iron Skillet Supper

Makes 6 servings.

- 1 pound ground beef
- 1 medium onion, chopped
- ½ green pepper, chopped
- 1 16-ounce can kidney beans, drained
- 2 tomatoes, chopped
- 1 8-ounce jar processed American cheese
- 2 teaspoons chili powder
- Corn chips

Brown beef in a frying pan; drain fat. Add onion and green pepper; sauté until tender. Stir in remaining ingredients, except chips. Simmer for 15 minutes. Sprinkle chips on top. Serve from skillet.

Mac Beef and Cheese

Makes 6 to 8 servings.

- 1 pound ground beef
- ½ onion, chopped
- 1 15½-ounce jar spaghetti sauce
- 2 cups elbow macaroni, cooked per package directions and drained
- 6 slices American or Cheddar cheese

Sauté beef and onion in a frying pan until brown; drain fat. Add ⅔ of the spaghetti sauce to the pan; simmer for 5 minutes. Combine beef mixture with macaroni. Pour into a casserole. Pour remaining sauce over top. Cut cheese slices diagonally in half; arrange around edge of casserole, facing points towards the center. Bake in a 350° oven for 10 minutes or until cheese is just melted.

Tortilla Casserole

Makes 6 to 8 servings.

- 1½ pounds ground beef
- 2 tablespoons vegetable oil
- 1 onion, chopped
- 1 rib celery, chopped
- 1 green pepper, chopped
- 1 cup raw rice
- 1 cup sliced black or green olives
- 1 28-ounce can tomatoes with liquid
- 1 cup water
- 2 teaspoons salt
- 2 to 3 tablespoons chili powder
- ¼ teaspoon black pepper
- 1 tablespoon Worcestershire sauce
- 1 cup crumbled corn chips
- 1 cup grated Cheddar cheese (about 4 ounces)

Brown ground beef in a frying pan; drain fat. Transfer to a large casserole. Heat oil in the same pan. Sauté onion, celery, green pepper, and rice for 3 to 4 minutes. Spoon over beef in casserole. Combine olives, tomatoes, water, salt, chili powder, pepper, and Worcestershire sauce; mix thoroughly. Pour over meat and vegetables; mix well. Sprinkle on corn chips and cheese. Cover and bake at 375° for 1 hour.

Pastitio

Makes 4 to 6 servings.

Meat Sauce

- 1 medium onion, chopped
- 2 tablespoons olive oil
- 1 pound ground beef
- 1 8-ounce can tomato sauce
- ½ teaspoon salt
- 1 clove garlic, crushed
- ½ teaspoon cinnamon

Sauté onion in oil until golden. Add beef and cook until brown; drain fat. Add tomato sauce, salt, garlic, and cinnamon. Simmer for 20 minutes.

Cream Sauce

- 2 tablespoons margarine
- 2 tablespoons flour
- 1½ cups milk
- 2 eggs, lightly beaten
- Dash salt, pepper, and nutmeg
- 1 teaspoon cinnamon

Melt margarine in a small saucepan. Stir in flour. Heat until bubbly, stirring constantly. Gradually add milk. Stir until smooth. Simmer for 5 minutes or until thickened, stirring constantly. Remove from heat; cool slightly. Slowly add eggs to half of the cream sauce, beating constantly. Return egg mixture to remaining sauce in pan; blend well. Season with salt, pepper, nutmeg, and cinnamon.

Assemble

- ½ pound elbow macaroni, cooked and drained
- ½ cup grated Cheddar cheese (about 2 ounces)

Place half of the macaroni in a greased 8-inch square baking dish. Spread Meat Sauce evenly over macaroni. Add remaining macaroni. Pour on Cream Sauce. Sprinkle on cheese. Bake in a 350° oven for 35 to 40 minutes or until custard is firm. Let stand for 10 minutes before serving.

Noodles and Beef Casserole

Makes 4 to 6 servings.

- 1 pound ground beef
- ½ onion, chopped
- 2 8-ounce cans tomato sauce or tomato sauce with mushrooms
- 1 teaspoon salt
- ¼ teaspoon black pepper
- ¼ teaspoon cinnamon
- 8 ounces medium noodles, cooked and drained
- 1 cup cottage cheese
- ½ cup shredded Cheddar cheese

Brown beef and onion in a frying pan; drain fat. Stir in 1 can of the tomato sauce, salt, pepper, and cinnamon. Pour into a shallow casserole. Arrange noodles around the edges. Top with cottage cheese. Sprinkle on shredded cheese. Pour on remaining can of tomato sauce. Bake at 350° for 30 minutes.

Lasagna

Makes 8 to 10 servings.

Meat Sauce

- 1 pound ground beef
- 1 clove garlic, minced
- 1 tablespoon parsley flakes
- 1 tablespoon crushed basil
- 1½ teaspoons salt
- 1 1-pound can tomatoes
- 2 6-ounce cans tomato paste

Brown beef in a large saucepan; drain fat. Add remaining ingredients. Simmer 30 minutes, stirring occasionally. Prepare Cheese Filling.

Cheese Filling

- 3 cups small curd, creamed cottage cheese
- 2 eggs, lightly beaten
- 2 tablespoons parsley flakes
- 1 teaspoon salt
- ½ teaspoon black pepper
- ½ cup grated Parmesan cheese

Combine all ingredients; mix thoroughly. Set aside.

Assemble

- 1 package lasagna noodles, cooked per package directions, rinsed in cold water, and drained
- 1 pound mozzarella cheese, thinly sliced and cut in half diagonally

Place half of the cooked noodles in a 9 x 13-inch baking dish. Spread half of the Cheese Filling, half of the mozzarella cheese, and half of the Meat Sauce over the noodles. Repeat layers, ending with Meat Sauce. Decorate top with triangles of mozzarella. Bake in a 375° oven for 30 minutes. Let stand 10 to 15 minutes before serving. Cut into squares, if desired.

Beef and Cheese Bake

Makes 10 to 12 servings.

- 1½ pounds ground beef
- 2 8-ounce cans tomato sauce
  Dash Worcestershire sauce
- ¼ teaspoon sugar
- 1 teaspoon salt
- 1 cup cream-style cottage cheese
- ½ cup sour cream or sour half-and-half
- 8 ounces cream cheese, softened
- ½ cup snipped green onions
- ¼ cup chopped green pepper
- 8 ounces medium noodles, cooked and drained
- ¼ cup grated Parmesan cheese

Sauté beef until brown; drain fat. Add tomato sauce, Worcestershire sauce, sugar, and salt. Remove from heat. Combine cottage cheese, sour cream, and cream cheese. Add onion and green pepper. Lightly oil a 9 x 13-inch baking dish. Spread half of the noodles on the bottom. Spoon a little of the meat sauce over the noodles. Cover with cheese mixture. Top with remaining noodles. Spoon on remaining meat sauce. Sprinkle on Parmesan cheese. Bake at 350° for 45 minutes or until bubbly hot.

Mexican Goulash

Makes 18 to 20 servings.

- 2 pounds pinto beans, washed
- 5 pounds ground beef
- 10 to 12 onions, chopped
- 2 tablespoons butter
- 2 tablespoons vegetable oil
- 2 tablespoons salt
- 4 tablespoons chili powder
  Tabasco sauce to taste
  Ground cumin to taste
- 2 28-ounce cans tomatoes
- 6 green peppers, cut into strips

Place beans in a large kettle. Cover with water. Cook slowly for 2½ hours or until beans are tender; drain. Brown beef in a frying pan; drain fat. Sauté onions in butter and oil until just tender. Combine beef, onions, seasonings, tomatoes, and green peppers. Simmer for 30 minutes. Stir in beans and heat through. Correct seasonings.

Combination Pizza Pie

Makes 4 to 8 servings.

- 1 can sliced mushrooms, drained, reserve liquid
- 1 egg, lightly beaten
- 2 slices bread, crusts removed, and bread crumbled
- ½ teaspoon oregano
- ½ teaspoon salt
- ¼ teaspoon black pepper
- 1 pound ground beef, or combination of beef, veal and pork
- 8 slices mozzarella cheese, cut diagonally in half
- 1 8-ounce jar pizza sauce
- ½ onion, chopped

Add water to mushroom liquid to equal ⅓ cup. Combine mushroom liquid, egg, bread, oregano, salt, and pepper; let stand for 4 to 5 minutes. Add beef and mix well. Pat into a 9-inch pie plate. Place half of the cheese over the meat. Spoon pizza sauce over cheese. Sprinkle on mushrooms and onion. Bake at 350° for 45 to 60 minutes. Top with remaining cheese and bake 5 to 10 minutes or until cheese is golden.

Anchovy Pizza

Makes 4 servings.

- 1 12 to 14-inch pizza crust
- ½ pound ground beef
- 1 clove garlic, crushed
- 3 tomatoes, sliced
- 8 ounces mozzarella cheese, sliced
- 1 can anchovies, drained and minced, reserve oil
- 1 can pitted ripe olives, drained and sliced
- 1 teaspoon crushed basil

Prepare crust. Preheat oven to 425°. Sauté beef and garlic until meat is no longer red; drain fat. Spread all ingredients over crust. Drizzle anchovy oil over all. Bake for 30 minutes or until crisp and golden.

Skillet Steak and Eggs

Makes 2 servings.

- ½ pound ground beef
- 1 small onion, chopped
- 1 10-ounce package frozen chopped spinach, thawed and drained, optional
- 2 eggs, lightly beaten
  Salt and pepper to taste

Brown beef in a frying pan over medium heat until just brown. Add onion and cook until tender; drain fat. Add spinach, if desired. Stir in eggs and scramble. Season with salt and pepper.

Hamburger Quiche

Makes 6 to 8 servings.

- ½ pound ground beef
- ½ onion, chopped
- ½ green pepper, chopped
- ½ cup mayonnaise
- ½ cup milk
- 2 eggs
- 1 tablespoon cornstarch
- ½ pound Cheddar or Swiss cheese, shredded
- 2 green onions, minced
- 1 unbaked, 9-inch pie shell

Brown beef, onion, and green pepper in a frying pan over medium heat; drain fat. Place in pie shell. Combine mayonnaise, milk, eggs, and cornstarch; mix until smooth. Stir in cheese and green onions. Pour into the pie shell. Bake at 350° for 35 to 40 minutes or until a knife inserted in the center comes out clean. Let stand 10 minutes before serving.

If you wish to avoid excess fat in meat loaves, place the loaf on a rack in a baking pan. Excess fat will drain into the pan below.

Picadillo

Makes 4 servings.

- 2 tablespoons vegetable oil
- 2 cloves garlic, minced
- 1 onion, chopped
- 1 pound ground beef
- ½ teaspoon ground cumin
  Salt and freshly ground pepper to taste
- ½ cup dry red wine
- 2 tomatoes, peeled, seeded and chopped or 1 8-ounce can tomato sauce
- ½ cup raisins, soaked in warm water for 20 minutes and drained
- ½ cup pimiento-stuffed olives, halved
- 1 green pepper, cut into julienne strips

Heat oil in a frying pan. Sauté garlic and onion until soft and golden. Add beef, cumin, salt, and pepper. Cook and stir for 5 minutes. Add wine, tomatoes, raisins, and olives. Cover and simmer for 15 minutes. Add green pepper and cook for 2 minutes. Serve with rice.

Note: To increase the serving number, add 2 cubed and cooked potatoes and ½ cup frozen green peas.

Kokletin

Makes 12 servings.

    1 slice rye bread, crust trimmed
    ¼ cup water
    2 pounds ground beef
    1 onion, grated
    3 cloves garlic, minced
    2 eggs, lightly beaten
    2 teaspoons salt
    ½ teaspoon freshly ground black pepper
    ¼ cup vegetable oil

Soak bread in water until water is absorbed. Squeeze out excess. Tear bread into pieces. Combine all ingredients, except oil; mix well. Shape into 12 oval patties. Heat oil in a frying pan. Fry patties for 10 minutes on each side or until well done. Serve with fried potatoes.

Spaghetti Lucania

Makes 4 servings.

    1 pound ground beef
    1 medium onion, chopped
    2 cloves garlic, minced
    3 tablespoons olive oil
    1 1-pound can tomatoes
    1 6-ounce can tomato paste
    ¼ teaspoon oregano
    ⅛ teaspoon thyme
    ⅛ teaspoon basil
    ½ cup sweet vermouth

Brown beef in a frying pan; drain fat. Sauté onion and garlic in oil until golden. Add beef, tomatoes, tomato paste, oregano, thyme, basil, and vermouth. Simmer until smooth and thick, about 35 minutes. Serve over cooked spaghetti. Serve with grated Parmesan cheese. Makes enough sauce for 1 pound cooked spaghetti.

Bolognese Sauce

Makes 4 servings.

    2 slices bacon, cut into small pieces
    1 onion, chopped
    1 clove garlic, crushed
    1 carrot, diced
    1 rib celery, diced
    ½ pound ground beef or veal
    1 6-ounce can tomato paste
    1 cup bouillon
    1 teaspoon oregano
    ½ bay leaf
    ½ cup grated Parmesan cheese

Sauté bacon in frying pan. Add onion, garlic, carrot, celery, and beef; cook until vegetables are tender and beef is no longer red; drain fat. Add tomato paste, bouillon, and herbs. Simmer for 30 minutes. Serve over cooked spaghetti. Sprinkle on cheese just before serving. Makes enough sauce for 1 pound cooked spaghetti.

Spanish Beef and Rice

Makes 6 to 8 servings.

    ¼ cup vegetable oil
    1½ cups long grain rice
    1 clove garlic, minced
    ½ onion, minced
    1 16-ounce can tomatoes
    1 6-ounce can tomato paste
    1 small bay leaf
    1 teaspoon salt
    3 to 4 drops Tabasco sauce
    4 cups hot water
    1½ pounds ground beef
    1 teaspoon chili powder
    ½ teaspoon sugar
    1 10¾-ounce can beef broth or consomme

Heat oil in a large frying pan. Add rice; stir until rice is golden brown. Add garlic and onion; sauté until golden. Stir in tomatoes, tomato paste, bay leaf, salt, Tabasco, and water. Cover and simmer for 15 minutes. Brown ground beef in another frying pan; drain fat. Stir in chili powder, sugar, and beef broth. Combine meat and rice mixture. Simmer for 40 to 60 minutes. Add more water or tomato juice to prevent sticking, if necessary.

Quick Spanish Beef and Rice

Makes 6 servings.

    1 pound ground beef
    1 onion, chopped
    1 green pepper, cut into ¾-inch cubes
    1 cup uncooked rice
    1 15-ounce can tomato sauce with tomato bits
    2 cups hot water
    ½ teaspoon sugar
       Salt and pepper to taste
       Grated sharp Cheddar cheese

In a frying pan, brown beef, onion, and green pepper; drain fat. Add rice, tomato sauce, water, sugar, salt, and pepper. Bring to a boil. Cover tightly and simmer for 25 minutes. Serve with a bowl of grated cheese.

Cantonese Beef

Makes 4 servings.

- 1 9-ounce package frozen French-style green beans
- ¾ pound ground beef
- 1 onion, chopped
- 1 clove garlic, minced
- ¼ cup soy sauce
- ½ teaspoon sugar
- 2 tablespoons water
- 1 cup cooked rice
- 2 eggs, lightly beaten
- 1 cup bean sprouts, optional

Thaw green beans; separate and drain. In a heated frying pan or wok, stir-fry beef, onion, and garlic until meat is browned and onion is tender, leaving meat in large chunks. Drain fat. Stir in soy sauce, sugar, and water. Remove meat from pan. Stir-fry green beans for 2 minutes. Add rice; cook and stir for 2 minutes. Stir-fry eggs in the center of the pan. Return meat to pan. Mix lightly. Stir in sprouts. Cook 1 to 2 minutes.

Cuban Beef

Makes 12 to 16 servings.

- ½ cup olive oil
- 4 onions, minced
- 2 cloves garlic, minced
- 4 green peppers, cut into julienne strips
- 2 6-ounce cans tomato paste
- 4 ounces raisins
- ½ cup whole or slivered, blanched almonds
- ¾ cup chopped ripe olives
- ¼ cup chopped green olives
- 4 pounds ground beef
- 2 cups beef bouillon or consomme

Combine all ingredients in a deep roaster. Cook at 325° for 2 to 3 hours; stir occasionally. Serve with rice.

Ginger Beef

Makes 3 to 4 servings.

- 1 pound ground beef
- 2 tablespoons soy sauce
- 2 tablespoons sherry wine
- 4 teaspoons cornstarch, divided
- 2 tablespoons cold water
- 3 cups finely shredded lettuce
- 1 tablespoon vegetable oil
- 3 green onions, thinly sliced
- 1 cup frozen green peas, thawed
- 1 teaspoon ground ginger
- 2 tablespoons chili sauce or catsup

In a mixing bowl, combine beef, soy sauce, sherry, and 2 teaspoons of the cornstarch. Mix remaining 2 teaspoons cornstarch in the cold water; set aside. Arrange the lettuce on a serving platter. In a heavy frying pan or wok, heat oil over high heat for 1 minute. Add beef mixture; cook and stir until browned. Add green onions, peas, ginger, and chili sauce; stir-fry for 1 minute. Stir cornstarch and water into pan. Cook about 30 seconds, stirring constantly until mixture is shiny. Spoon mixture over lettuce. Serve with rice.

Beef Oriental

Makes 2 to 4 servings.

- 1 pound ground beef
- 1 onion, chopped
- 2 ribs celery, sliced
- 1 can water chestnuts, sliced
- ½ to 1 cup fresh or canned bean sprouts (drained, if canned)
- ½ cup consomme or instant beef bouillon
- 2 tablespoons soy sauce
- 2 tablespoons catsup

Sauté beef until brown in a frying pan. Add onion and celery and sauté for 3 to 4 minutes. Stir in water chestnuts, bean sprouts, consomme, soy sauce, and catsup. Heat through. Serve over rice or Chinese noodles.

Mandarin Meatballs

Makes 6 servings.

- 1 pound ground beef
- 1 egg
- ¼ cup dry bread crumbs
- 2 tablespoons milk
- 1 teaspoon salt
- 2 tablespoons vegetable oil
- 2 tablespoons cornstarch
- 1 beef bouillon cube, crushed
- 1 tablespoon soy sauce
- 1 13½-ounce can pineapple chunks, drain, reserve ¾ cup liquid
- ¼ cup cider vinegar
- 1 11-ounce can mandarin oranges, drained

Combine beef, egg, bread crumbs, milk, and salt. Shape into 30 1-inch balls. Heat oil in a frying pan. Brown meatballs in oil on all sides. Remove from pan; set aside. Add cornstarch, bouillon, and soy sauce to drippings; stir for 1 to 2 minutes. Add pineapple liquid and vinegar. Bring to a boil; reduce heat to a simmer. Add meatballs, pineapple, and mandarin oranges. Heat through. Serve over hot rice.

Spaghetti Squash

Makes 4 servings.

- 1 spaghetti squash
- 1 pound ground beef
- 1 clove garlic, crushed
- 1 onion, chopped
- 1 6-ounce can tomato paste
- 1 1-pound can tomatoes
- 1 teaspoon salt
- ½ teaspoon sugar
- 1 teaspoon oregano
- 1 teaspoon crushed basil
- ½ cup grated Parmesan cheese

Lightly grease outside of squash. Bake at 350° for 1 hour, until soft to the touch. Cut in half lengthwise, remove seeds, and shred into "spaghetti" with a fork. Sauté beef, garlic, and onion until beef is no longer red; drain fat. Add remaining ingredients. Simmer for 15 minutes. Spoon into squash halves. Bake at 350° for 30 to 45 minutes. Serve in shells.

Chili-Stuffed Green Peppers

Makes 2 to 4 servings.

- 4 large green peppers, stems removed, hollowed out
- 1 cup minced onion
- 1 large clove garlic, minced
- 1 tablespoon vegetable oil
- ¾ pound ground beef
- 1 tablespoon chili powder
- ½ teaspoon ground cumin
- ½ teaspoon ground coriander
- ¼ teaspoon dried red pepper flakes
  Salt and pepper to taste
- 2 tablespoons tomato paste
- 1 cup macaroni, cooked and drained

Carefully cut off a thin slice from the bottom of each pepper so it will stand. Sauté onion and garlic in oil until tender. Add beef; brown, breaking it up with a spoon. Add chili powder, cumin, coriander, pepper flakes, salt, pepper, and tomato paste. Cook about 15 minutes, stirring often. Stir in cooked macaroni. Remove from heat. Bring a large kettle of water to a boil. Add green peppers; return water to a boil; simmer for about 2 minutes. Drain peppers well. Lightly grease a baking dish. Spoon meat mixture into the peppers. Stand peppers in dish. Bake at 375° for 35 minutes.

Stuffed Peppers

Makes 6 servings.

- 6 green peppers
- 1 pound ground beef, veal, pork or a combination
- ¼ cup uncooked rice
- 1 onion, grated
- 2 teaspoons salt
- ½ teaspoon freshly ground black pepper
- 1 egg, beaten with 3 tablespoons cold water
- 3 tablespoons vegetable oil or butter or combination
- 2 onions, sliced
- 1 28-ounce can tomatoes
- 2 teaspoons instant beef bouillon
- ¼ cup brown sugar
- ¼ cup lemon juice

Place peppers in a large saucepan; cover with water. Bring to a boil; remove from heat and let stand for 5 minutes; drain. Cut a 1-inch slice from the stem end; reserve. Remove seeds. Combine beef and rice; mix well. Add grated onion, 1½ teaspoons of the salt, ¼ teaspoon of the pepper, egg and water; mix well. Spoon mixture into peppers. Replace the tops. Heat oil in a deep frying pan. Sauté the sliced onions until golden. Place peppers on top of onions. Cut a very thin slice from the bottom so that peppers stand. Add tomatoes, bouillon, and remaining salt and pepper. Cover and cook over low heat for 1 hour.* Stir in brown sugar and lemon juice. Cook 30 minutes longer, until peppers are tender. Correct seasonings.

*May be baked in a 350° oven for 60 minutes or until peppers are tender.

Green Bean and Beef Bake

Makes 4 servings.

- 1 pound ground beef
- ½ teaspoon salt
- ¼ teaspoon black pepper
- 1 tablespoon bottled steak sauce
- 2 10-ounce packages frozen green beans, separated
- 1 10¾-ounce can cream of mushroom, chicken or celery soup
- ½ cup milk
- 1 3-ounce can French fried onion rings

Brown beef until no longer red; drain fat. Add remaining ingredients, except onion rings; blend thoroughly. Pour into a lightly greased casserole. Bake in a 350° oven for 20 minutes or until bubbly. Spread onion rings on top. Bake 5 to 10 minutes or until onions are crisp.

Stuffed Cabbage Rolls

Makes 6 servings.

 1 pound ground beef
¼ pound ground pork
 2 teaspoons salt
½ teaspoon black pepper
¾ cup cooked rice
 1 small onion, minced
 2 8-ounce cans tomato sauce with tomato bits
12 large cabbage leaves, blanched 2 to 3 minutes
    and drained
¼ cup packed brown sugar
¼ cup lemon juice

Combine beef, pork, salt, pepper, rice, onion, and 1 can of the tomato sauce; mix thoroughly. Divide meat mixture among cabbage leaves, placing mixture in the center of each leaf. Fold sides in to the middle; roll up. Place in a casserole, seam-sides down. Combine remaining can of tomato sauce with brown sugar and lemon juice. Pour over cabbage rolls. Cover and simmer for 30 minutes. Remove cover, baste, and simmer 30 minutes.

Stuffed Potato Balls

Makes 4 servings.

½ cup butter or margarine
 1 small onion, minced
½ pound ground beef
½ pound ground pork
½ cup dry bread crumbs
⅓ cup cream
 1 tablespoon snipped parsley
 1 tablespoon crushed tarragon
½ teaspoon salt
¼ teaspoon black pepper
 4 cups prepared instant mashed potatoes, made
    without adding milk
 4 ounces grated Parmesan cheese
 1 cup dry bread crumbs

Heat 1 tablespoon of the butter in a small frying pan. Sauté onion until tender. Combine onion, meat, the ½ cup bread crumbs, cream, and all seasonings; mix thoroughly. Shape into 16 balls. Fry in 2 tablespoons of the butter for about 20 minutes, turning to brown all sides. Remove from pan. Cover each ball with mashed potatoes. Carefully roll in cheese and the 1 cup of bread crumbs. Butter a baking pan with remaining butter. Place meatballs in pan. Bake at 350° for 15 minutes or until golden.

Cheese-Topped Stuffed Peppers

Makes 4 to 6 servings.

 6 green peppers
¼ cup chopped onion
 1 tablespoon butter plus 1 tablespoon vegetable oil
 1 pound ground chuck
½ cup cooked rice
½ teaspoon salt
¼ teaspoon black pepper
 2 8-ounce cans tomato sauce
½ cup sour cream or sour half-and-half
¼ cup sherry
¼ pound sharp Cheddar cheese, grated or shredded

Remove stem ends and seeds from peppers. Sauté onion in butter and oil. Add beef and brown. Stir in rice, salt, pepper, and 1 can of the tomato sauce. Spoon mixture into peppers. Stand peppers in a baking dish. Combine sour cream, the remaining can of tomato sauce, and sherry; pour over peppers. Bake in a preheated 350° oven for 45 to 60 minutes. Sprinkle on cheese and bake 15 minutes or until cheese is golden.

To insure that green peppers will not be bitter, simply blanch before filling.

Do not refreeze ground meat once it has been thawed.

Potato Boats

Makes 12 boats.

 6 large baking potatoes
 1 pound ground beef
 1 onion, minced
 1 teaspoon salt
½ teaspoon black pepper
 2 teaspoons beef bouillon crystals
 1 cup sour half-and-half

Scrub potatoes; pierce skin with a fork. Bake at 375° for 50 to 60 minutes until fork-tender. Cut in half and scoop out; reserve. Brown beef and onion in a large frying pan; drain fat. Mash potato lightly with a fork. Season with salt and pepper. Stir potato into meat mixture. Heap into potato shells. Place in a casserole. Mix bouillon crystals into sour half-and-half. Spoon over potato boats. Bake at 350° for 30 to 40 minutes until steaming hot.

Lamb Burgers

Makes 4 servings.

    3 slices bread, crusts trimmed
    ¼ cup cold water or white wine
    1 pound ground lamb
    ½ onion, grated
    1 clove garlic, minced
    2 tablespoons catsup
      Salt and pepper to taste
    1 egg, lightly beaten
    1 tablespoon snipped parsley

Soak bread in water or wine until water is absorbed. Combine bread with remaining ingredients; mix well. Shape into 4 large burgers. Place in a lightly greased pan. Bake at 375° or until tops are browned. Serve on a bed of rice.

Lamb Spanakopitta

Spinach Pie with Lamb

Makes 8 servings.

    1 small onion, chopped
    2 tablespoons butter
    ¼ cup minced scallions
    2 10-ounce packages frozen, chopped spinach,
      thawed and thoroughly drained
    2 tablespoons minced parsley
    1 teaspoon dillweed
    1 teaspoon salt
    ¼ teaspoon black pepper
    ¼ cup milk
    ¼ pound feta cheese, coarsely crumbled
    3 eggs, lightly beaten
    1 cup butter, melted
    ½ pound phyllo pastry
    ½ pound ground lamb, cooked and drained

Sauté onion in the 2 tablespoons butter until golden brown. Add scallions and cook until wilted. Add spinach and seasonings; toss lightly. Remove from heat; add milk. Combine feta cheese with eggs. Add to spinach mixture; mix well. Use a pastry brush to coat bottom and sides of a 9 x 13-inch baking dish with melted butter. Line with 8 sheets of phyllo, brushing each sheet with melted butter. Do not trim overhanging sections. Pour in spinach mixture. Crumble lamb over top of spinach. Fold overhanging phyllo back over filling. Top with 8 sheets of phyllo, brushing each sheet with butter. Brush top with butter. Score into squares or diamonds. Bake at 350° for 45 minutes. Let stand 10 minutes before serving.

Greek Patties

Makes 4 to 6 servings.

    1 pound ground lamb
    ½ cup fresh bread crumbs
    ½ teaspoon salt
    1 onion, minced
    2 tablespoons chopped parsley
    1 tablespoon chopped mint
    1 egg, lightly beaten
    2 tablespoons anise-flavored liqueur

Combine all ingredients; mix well. Form into 4 to 6 meat patties. Broil for 4 to 6 minutes on each side, until brown.

Greek Lamb and Cabbage Stew

Makes 4 to 5 servings.

    8 to 10 ground lamb patties, broiled and drained
    ½ cup barley
    4 cups chicken broth
    1 small head cabbage, cut into 8 wedges
    1 16-ounce can tomatoes
    1 large tart apple, diced
    ¼ cup raisins
    2 tablespoons brown sugar
    2 tablespoons lemon juice

Combine barley and broth in a saucepan. Bring to a simmer; cook for 20 minutes. Add vegetables, fruits, brown sugar, and lemon juice. Cook for 20 minutes. Just before serving, add broiled lamb patties; heat to steaming.

Lamb and Mushroom Muffins

Makes 8 servings.

    2 tablespoons butter or margarine
    1 clove garlic, minced
    1 onion, minced
    ½ pound mushrooms, sliced
    1 cup sour half-and-half
    1 teaspoon paprika
    1 teaspoon lemon juice
    8 lamb patties, broiled
    4 English muffins, split, toasted, and buttered

Melt butter in a saucepan. Sauté garlic, onion, and mushrooms until tender. Stir in sour half-and-half, paprika, and lemon juice. Heat to steaming. Broil lamb patties to desired doneness. Place a lamb pattie on each muffin half. Spoon sour cream and mushroom gravy over each.

Skillet Lamb

Makes 8 servings.

- 2 pounds ground lamb
- ½ cup chopped onion
- 1 clove garlic, minced
- 1 eggplant, pared and cubed
- 1 14-ounce jar spaghetti sauce
- 2 teaspoons salt
- ⅛ teaspoon black pepper
- 1 teaspoon basil
- 6 ounces mozzarella cheese, sliced and cut into strips
- 6 ripe olives, sliced
  Minced parsley

Brown lamb in a frying pan, breaking it into chunks. Push to one side of pan. Sauté onion and garlic in drippings until tender. Drain fat. Stir in eggplant, spaghetti sauce, and seasonings. Cover and bring to a boil. Reduce heat and simmer for 20 minutes or until eggplant is tender. Uncover. Arrange cheese in a lattice pattern on top of mixture. Place 1 or 2 olive slices in the space between cheese strips. Cover and simmer for 3 minutes or until cheese begins to melt. Sprinkle on parsley. Serve from frying pan.

Dolmathes me Augolemono

Makes 6 to 8 servings.

- 1 tablespoon olive oil
- 1 large onion, chopped
- 1 clove garlic, crushed
- 1 large tomato, peeled and chopped
- ¼ cup snipped parsley
- 1 tablespoon chopped fresh mint, or 1 teaspoon dried
- 1 pound ground beef
- 1 pound ground lamb
- ½ cup raw rice
- 1½ teaspoons salt
- ¼ teaspoon black pepper
- 2 small heads green cabbage
- 1 10½-ounce can beef bouillon

Heat olive oil in a saucepan. Sauté onion, garlic, and tomato until tender. Stir in parsley and mint. Combine onion-tomato mixture with beef, lamb, rice, salt, and pepper. Set aside. Place cabbage, 1 at a time, in a kettle of boiling water. Remove whole leaves as they soften. Each head yields 8 to 9 leaves. Make a slit in the center stalk of each leaf. Place 2 tablespoons meat mixture on each leaf. Fold sides of leaves in over filling and roll up. Arrange rolls, seam-side down, in a deep

saucepan. Add bouillon. Place a heatproof plate over cabbage rolls. Cover and cook 45 minutes to 1 hour. Remove rolls and keep warm. Save liquid for sauce. Prepare sauce. Pour over cabbage rolls.

Sauce

- 1 tablespoon cornstarch
- 1 tablespoon water
- 3 eggs
- ¼ cup lemon juice
- ½ teaspoon salt

Blend cornstarch and water. Pour into boiling bouillon from above. Boil for 1 minute. Beat eggs until lemony. Beat in lemon juice and salt. Gradually add hot sauce, stirring constantly. Return to pan and heat until slightly thickened; do not boil. Pour over cabbage rolls.

Florentine Lamb Casserole

Makes 4 to 6 servings.

- 1 pound ground lamb
- 1 onion, chopped
- 1 clove garlic, minced
- 1 8-ounce package shell macaroni, cooked and drained
- 1 10-ounce package frozen, chopped spinach, thawed and drained
- ½ cup grated Swiss cheese
- ½ cup milk
- 2 tablespoons tomato paste
- ½ teaspoon salt
- ½ teaspoon rosemary
- ¼ teaspoon black pepper

Brown lamb, onion, and garlic until lamb is brown; drain fat. Combine with remaining ingredients; mix well. Turn into a greased, 2-quart casserole. Bake at 350° for 30 to 40 minutes.

Zucchini Boats

Makes 20 filled boats.

- 10 small zucchini
- 1 pound ground lamb
- 3 tomatoes, chopped
- 2 small onions, chopped
- 1 cup canned chick peas (garbanzos)
- ½ cup pine nuts
- 1 teaspoon salt
- 1 teaspoon curry powder
- 3 tablespoons vinegar
- 1 cup grated Parmesan cheese

Slice zucchini in half lengthwise. Scoop out pulp; chop and reserve. Set shells aside. Sauté lamb, zucchini pulp, tomatoes, onions, chick peas, pine nuts, salt, and curry powder until lamb is no longer pink. Stir in vinegar and cheese. Fill shells with mixture. Chill. Serve chilled as a first course.

Stuffed Tomatoes with Curried Lamb

Makes 4 to 8 servings.

    8 firm tomatoes
    1 pound ground lean lamb
    ½ cup minced celery
    1 clove garlic, minced
    ½ cup minced onion
    2 tablespoons butter or margarine
    1 to 2 tablespoons curry powder
      Salt and pepper to taste
    ¼ cup fine bread crumbs

Slice tops off tomatoes; scoop out pulp leaving a thick shell. Chop the tomato pulp and reserve. Brown lamb; drain and set aside. Sauté celery, garlic, and onion in butter. Add tomato pulp, curry powder, salt, and pepper. Stir often, breaking up meat. Stuff the tomatoes with the lamb curry. Arrange in a baking dish. Spoon bread crumbs on top of each tomato. Bake in a 350° oven for 30 minutes.

Curried Lamb Loaf

Makes 6 servings.

    4 slices bread, crusts trimmed
    ½ cup cold milk or water
    1½ pounds ground lamb
    1 small onion, grated
    1 small carrot, grated
      Salt and pepper to taste
    1 to 2 teaspoons curry powder
    2 eggs, lightly beaten
    ¼ cup white wine
    1 tablespoon snipped parsley

Soak bread in milk until liquid is absorbed. Combine bread with remaining ingredients in a mixing bowl; mix well. Place mixture in a greased 9 x 5-inch loaf pan. Bake at 375° for 1 hour or until loaf is brown and firm to the touch. Serve with broiled pineapple slices, chutney, or curry condiments such as salted nuts, coconut, snipped green onions, raisins, chopped hard-cooked egg, mandarin orange segments, or chopped, cooked bacon.

Lemon-Lamb Meatballs

Makes 4 servings.

    1 pound ground lamb or ½ beef and ½ lamb
    ⅔ cup chopped parsley
    ½ cup cracker crumbs
    1 small onion, minced
    ¼ cup milk
    ½ teaspoon salt
    ¼ teaspoon black pepper
    ¼ teaspoon rosemary
    ½ teaspoon grated lemon peel
    1 teaspoon vegetable oil
    1 cup chicken broth
    1 tablespoon lemon juice
    1 tablespoon cornstarch
    1 tablespoon water

Combine lamb, parsley, cracker crumbs, onion, milk, seasonings, and lemon peel. Shape into 2-inch meatballs. Heat oil in a frying pan. Brown meatballs on all sides; drain. Add broth. Cover and simmer for 10 minutes. Mix lemon juice, cornstarch, and water to a smooth paste. Add to pan. Cook and stir for 2 to 3 minutes, until sauce thickens and becomes clear. Serve over rice.

Lamb and Rice Pilaf

Makes 6 servings.

    2 tablespoons butter or margarine
    2 tablespoons vegetable oil
    3 onions, chopped
    1 clove garlic, minced
    1 pound ground lamb or lean beef
    ⅓ cup pine nuts
    ⅓ cup raisins, plumped in warm water, drained
    2 cups rice
    4 cups beef bouillon
    2 tomatoes, peeled, seeded and chopped
    2 tablespoons snipped parsley
    ½ teaspoon coriander
    ½ teaspoon cinnamon
      Salt and freshly ground black pepper to taste

Heat butter and oil in a heavy frying pan. Sauté onions and garlic until soft and golden. Add lamb; cook and stir for 5 minutes; drain fat. Add nuts and raisins; cook and stir for 2 minutes. Add rice and stir for 5 minutes. Add bouillon, tomatoes, parsley, and seasonings. Cover and simmer over low heat for 40 minutes or until rice is tender. Remove from heat and spoon into a heated serving dish. Cover with a napkin and let stand for 10 minutes to allow moisture to absorb into napkin.

Curried Lamb

Makes 6 to 8 servings.

2 pounds ground lamb
2 slices raisin bread, trimmed and torn into pieces
1 apple, chopped
½ cup milk
1 tablespoon curry powder
1 teaspoon salt
½ teaspoon black pepper
1 tablespoon vegetable oil
1 tablespoon flour
½ to ¾ cup chicken broth

Combine lamb, bread, apple, milk, and seasonings. Form into 2-inch balls. Press to flatten slightly. Heat oil in a frying pan. Brown meatballs; remove. Drain all but 1 tablespoon fat. Add flour and stir to make a smooth paste. Add chicken broth. Cook and stir until smooth. Return patties to sauce. Heat to bubbling. Serve with rice and condiments such as snipped green onions, chopped hard-boiled eggs, coconut, chopped peanuts or almonds, raisins, chopped green pepper, chutney. Use three or four—some sweet, some salty, some fruity.

Meatballs can be browned with no extra fat if they're placed on a lightly greased baking sheet and baked in a 350° oven for 15 minutes.

Lamb Navarin

Makes 8 to 12 servings.

 3 pounds ground lamb
 1 clove garlic, minced
 1 small onion, minced
 ½ teaspoon thyme
 1 egg, lightly beaten
 ½ cup fine bread crumbs
 2 tablespoons vegetable oil
 2 tablespoons flour
 1 10½-ounce can beef bouillon
 1 1-pound can tomatoes
 ½ teaspoon thyme
 ½ bay leaf
 ½ teaspoon rosemary
 2 tablespoons butter
12 small, whole, peeled onions
 4 small turnips, peeled and quartered
12 whole new potatoes
 4 carrots, cut into chunks
 1 10-ounce package frozen peas
 2 tablespoons snipped parsley

Combine lamb, garlic, onion, thyme, egg, and bread crumbs; mix well. Shape into 16 to 18 patties. Heat oil in a large frying pan. Brown 3 to 4 patties at a time. Drain off all but 2 tablespoons fat. Return patties to pan. Sprinkle on flour. Add bouillon, tomatoes, thyme, bay leaf, and rosemary. Simmer until thickened, stirring frequently. While lamb patties and sauce are cooking, melt butter in another frying pan. Sauté vegetables, except peas, until golden. Add to lamb. Cover and simmer for 20 to 30 minutes, until vegetables are tender. Add peas the last 10 minutes of cooking time. Remove bay leaf. Garnish with parsley before serving.

Dolmades

Stuffed Grape Leaves

Makes 8 to 10 servings.

 1 tablespoon salt
 1 pint jar grape leaves
 2 pounds ground lamb
 1 onion, chopped
 1 clove garlic, minced
 2 teaspoons salt
 ½ teaspoon black pepper
 ½ cup raw rice
 ½ cup snipped parsley
1½ cups water
 4 tablespoons butter

Bring 1 quart water to a boil. Add the 1 tablespoon salt and grape leaves. Return to a boil; cover and cook for 10 minutes, separating leaves with a fork. Remove from heat and drain. Combine lamb and remaining ingredients, except butter; mix well. Spoon 1 teaspoon of the meat mixture onto the rough side of a grape leaf; roll up. Fill all leaves and place in a large kettle, one layer on top of another. Dot top with butter. Cover with boiling water. Cover and simmer for 1½ hours. Drain liquid from kettle; keep dolmades in kettle. Prepare Lemon Sauce. Pour sauce over dolmades in kettle; lightly shake kettle to distribute the sauce. Let stand 5 to 10 minutes before serving.

Lemon Sauce

2 eggs
3 tablespoons lemon juice
  Liquid from Dolmades, above

Beat eggs until light and fluffy. Add lemon juice. Slowly add liquid from Dolmades, beating constantly.

Corned Beef

Reubens

Makes 8 open-face sandwiches.

   1 tablespoon butter
   1 12-ounce can corned beef, chopped
   1 small onion, minced
   ½ cup mayonnaise
   1 tablespoon prepared mustard
   1 tablespoon horseradish
   8 slices rye bread, toasted on 1 side
   1 16-ounce can sauerkraut, drained
   8 slices Swiss cheese

Melt butter in a small frying pan. Sauté corned beef and onion until corned beef is crispy and onion is tender. Mix mayonnaise, mustard, and horseradish together. Spread on untoasted side of bread. Top with sauerkraut, corned beef, and 1 slice of cheese. Broil for 4 or 5 minutes until cheese is puffy and bubbly.

Corned Beef and Macaroni

Makes 4 to 6 servings.

   2 cups cooked macaroni
   1 12-ounce can corned beef, ground or shredded
   1 cup grated Cheddar cheese
   1 10¾-ounce can cream of mushroom soup
   ¼ cup milk
   ½ cup buttered bread crumbs

Combine all ingredients, except crumbs; mix well. Place in a greased casserole. Sprinkle on crumbs. Bake at 350° for 30 to 40 minutes until hot and bubbly.

Split Pea Soup

Makes 8 to 10 servings.

   1 pound dried split peas
   2 quarts chicken or turkey broth
   2 ribs celery, cut in pieces
   1 carrot, cut in pieces
   1 onion, chopped
   1 ham hock or smoked turkey wing
   2 cups chopped corned beef or ham
   ¼ cup sherry, optional

Place the first 6 ingredients in a soup kettle. Cover and simmer for 2 hours, until soup thickens. Remove bone. If desired, puree soup in a blender at this point. Add meat and sherry. Heat to steaming.

Corned Beef Barbecue

Makes 8 servings.

   1 12-ounce can corned beef, chopped
   ½ cup water
   ½ cup catsup
   ½ cup chili sauce
   1 tablespoon Worcestershire sauce
   1 tablespoon vinegar
   1 small onion, minced
   8 hamburger rolls, sliced and toasted
     Sliced dill pickle

Combine corned beef, water, catsup, chili sauce, Worcestershire sauce, vinegar, and onion. Simmer for about 20 minutes, stirring often. Spoon onto hamburger rolls. Garnish with pickle slices.

Corned Beef Hash Burgers

Makes 4 servings.

   1 15-ounce can corned beef hash, cut into 4 slices and broiled
   4 hamburger rolls, sliced
   4 tablespoons tomato paste
   4 slices Swiss cheese

Place a broiled hash burger on each roll. Top with a dollop of tomato paste and a slice of cheese. Broil until cheese melts. Top with other roll half. Serve with mustard and pickles.

Baked Stuffed Tomatoes

Makes 4 servings.

   1 15-ounce can corned beef hash
   1 small onion, minced
   1 egg, lightly beaten
   4 tomatoes, tops removed; scoop out pulp and seeds

Combine hash, onion, and egg. Heap into tomato shells. Bake at 350° for 20 to 25 minutes.

Red Flannel Hash

Makes 6 to 8 servings.

   2 1-pound cans corned beef hash
   1 1-pound can julienne beets, drained and patted dry
   1 tablespoon instant minced onion
     Dash Tabasco sauce

Break up corned beef with a fork. Add beets, onion, and Tabasco sauce. Press into a large, ungreased frying pan. Sauté slowly until crusty brown. Turn only once and brown other side.

Corned Beef Hash-Filled Peppers

Makes 4 servings.

2 green peppers
1 15-ounce can corned beef hash, broken up
  and crumbled with a fork
1 tablespoon cream

Blanch green peppers in boiling water for 5 minutes. Cool in icy water; drain. Cut each green pepper in half. Stir cream into hash. Fill pepper halves. Bake in a 350° oven for 20 minutes or until heated through. Serve with heated tomato or cheese soup as a sauce.

Ground meats should be handled as little as possible to keep them juicy and tender.

Corned Beef Hash with Eggs

Makes 4 servings.

1 15-ounce can corned beef hash, cut into
  1-inch thick slices
1 egg for each slice hash

Arrange hash slices in a buttered baking pan. Press a hollow in the center of each and break an egg into it. Cover and bake 25 minutes at 325° or until the egg white is firm.

Ground meats should not be refrigerated over two days. If frozen, use within two or three months.

Corned Beef Hash Casserole

Makes 6 servings.

1 large can refrigerator biscuits
1 cup plain yogurt
¼ cup minced green onion
2 teaspoons prepared mustard
2 15-ounce cans corned beef hash
2 tablespoons snipped parsley

Oil a 10 x 6-inch casserole. Press biscuits in to form a crust. Combine yogurt, onion, and mustard. Stir half of yogurt mixture into the hash. Spread it evenly over the crust. Spread remaining yogurt mixture evenly over top of hash. Sprinkle on parsley. Bake at 375° for 35 minutes or until crust is brown.

Corned Beef and Cheese

Makes 6 servings.

¼ cup shredded sharp Cheddar cheese
2 tablespoons mayonnaise
4 ounces corned beef, ground
¼ cup minced dill pickles
1 tablespoon grated onion
  Salt and pepper to taste
  Worcestershire sauce to taste
12 slices rye bread

Combine cheese and mayonnaise in a small bowl; cream until fluffy. Add corned beef, dill pickles, onion, salt, pepper, and Worcestershire sauce; blend thoroughly. Divide mixture among half of the bread slices. Top with remaining bread. If desired, garnish with lettuce and sliced tomato.

Hawaiian Hash

Makes 4 servings.

1 15-ounce can corned beef hash, cut into
  1-inch thick slices
1 can cranberry-orange relish, or
1 small jar process cheese spread, or
1 small can pineapple slices, drained

Panfry hash slices. Serve topped with your choice of cranberry-orange relish, cheese spread, or pan-fried pineapple slices.

Corned Beef and Cabbage Salad

Makes 4 servings.

¾ cup mayonnaise
2 tablespoons horseradish
2 tablespoons milk
1 tablespoon mustard
½ teaspoon salt
⅛ teaspoon black pepper
2 cups cubed, boiled potatoes, chilled
3 cups thinly sliced cabbage
1 cup grated carrot
  Cabbage leaves
½ pound corned beef, ground
4 ounces Swiss cheese, julienned

Combine mayonnaise, horseradish, milk, mustard, salt, and pepper in a large mixing bowl; blend thoroughly. Add potatoes, shredded cabbage, and carrot; toss to coat. Line a serving bowl with cabbage leaves. Spoon salad onto cabbage leaves. Sprinkle corned beef over top. Arrange cheese on top of corned beef.

Veal

Veal-Burgers Stroganoff

Makes 6 servings.

1½ pounds ground veal
1 slice bread, crumbled
¼ cup milk
1 teaspoon salt
½ teaspoon black pepper
1 teaspoon marjoram
2 tablespoons vegetable oil
½ pound mushrooms, sliced
2 tablespoons chopped parsley
2 tablespoons flour
1 cup chicken broth
½ cup sour half-and-half
1 tablespoon paprika

Combine veal, bread, milk, salt, pepper, and marjoram; mix thoroughly. Shape into 12 patties. Heat oil in a frying pan. Brown patties. Add mushrooms and parsley; sauté for 3 to 4 minutes. Blend flour into chicken broth. Stir into meatballs until gravy thickens. Just before serving, add sour half-and-half. Sprinkle paprika on top. Serve over rice or noodles.

Veal Tonnato

Makes 6 servings.

2 pounds ground veal
1 cup shredded carrots
1 cup sour cream
¼ cup minced onion
¼ cup bread crumbs or matzo meal
1½ teaspoons salt
¼ teaspoon black pepper
¼ teaspoon thyme
2 tablespoons vegetable oil
1 3¼-ounce can tuna fish, drained and flaked
½ cup dry white wine
1 tablespoon flour
1 teaspoon instant chicken bouillon

Combine veal, carrots, ½ cup of the sour cream, onion, crumbs, salt, pepper, and thyme; mix lightly. Shape into six ¾-inch thick patties. Heat oil in a frying pan.Sauté patties until browned, turning only once. In a blender container or food processor, combine tuna, wine, flour, and bouillon. Process until smooth. Pour over patties. Cover and simmer for 25 minutes, basting several times. Remove to a serving platter. Stir remaining ½ cup sour cream into sauce. Heat slowly until just heated. Spoon over patties.

Saltimbocca

Makes 4 servings.

1 cup minced onion
2 tablespoons butter or margarine
2 tablespoons vegetable oil
2 10-ounce packages frozen, chopped spinach, thawed and squeezed very dry
½ teaspoon salt
¼ teaspoon black pepper
Pinch nutmeg
¾ pound ground veal, shaped into 4 patties or 4 frozen veal patties
½ cup dry white wine
4 thin slices prosciutto ham

Sauté onion in 1 tablespoon of the butter and 1 tablespoon of the oil until golden brown. Stir in spinach, salt, pepper, and nutmeg. Cover and reduce heat. In another frying pan, heat remaining butter and oil. Quickly brown veal patties on both sides. Remove to a platter leaving 2 tablespoons drippings in pan. Uncover spinach and raise heat to evaporate moisture. Spoon into a shallow casserole or au gratin dish. Add wine to drippings in frying pan. Bring to a boil. Add ham slices and heat until they ruffle. Place a ham slice on each veal pattie. Boil wine mixture for a few minutes. Arrange veal patties with ham on spinach mixture. Pour wine sauce over all.

Veal Marengo

Makes 6 servings.

1 8-ounce package medium noodles, cooked and drained
2 tablespoons butter or margarine
1½ pounds ground veal, shaped into 6 to 8 patties
1 cup small whole mushrooms
1 package frozen baby onions
1 cup spaghetti sauce
1 1-pound can tomatoes
½ cup garlic croutons
2 tablespoons chopped parsley

Spread noodles in a lightly oiled, shallow baking dish. Melt butter in a frying pan. Sauté veal patties until lightly browned. Place on top of noodles. Toss mushrooms and onions in the same pan to brown. Sprinkle over patties. Add spaghetti sauce and tomatoes to pan and simmer for 10 minutes. Pour over all. Sprinkle with croutons. Bake at 375° for 20 minutes. Sprinkle on parsley.

Veal-Stuffed Bell Peppers

Makes 6 servings.

    6 large green peppers
    4 slices bread, crusts trimmed
    ½ cup milk or water
    1½ pounds ground veal
    1 tablespoon snipped parsley
    1 clove garlic, minced
    1 tablespoon Worcestershire sauce
    1 teaspoon salt
    ¼ teaspoon black pepper
    ½ onion, minced
    1 egg, lightly beaten
    1 10¾-ounce can tomato soup
    ½ cup cold water or ¼ cup sherry plus ¼ cup water
    1 teaspoon sugar
    1 teaspoon instant onion

Cut tops off peppers; remove seeds and membranes. Carefully cut a thin slice from the end of each pepper so it will stand. Place in boiling, salted water for 5 minutes; drain. Soak bread in the ½ cup milk or water; squeeze dry. Combine bread, veal, seasonings, onion, and egg. Spoon veal mixture into peppers. Place in a baking dish. Combine soup, water or sherry, sugar, and instant onion; blend thoroughly. Pour over peppers. Cover and bake at 350° for 35 minutes. Uncover and bake 15 minutes longer. Serve with rice.

Veal Burgers

Makes 6 servings.

    4 tablespoons vegetable oil, divided
    2 onions, chopped
    5 slices white bread, crusts trimmed
    ¾ cup boiling water
    1½ pounds ground veal
    1 teaspoon salt
    ½ teaspoon black pepper
    3 eggs
    1 cup bread crumbs

Heat 2 tablespoons of the oil in a frying pan. Sauté onion for 10 minutes. Soak bread in water. Squeeze out excess water; mash bread. Combine bread, veal, salt, pepper, 2 of the eggs, and onions; mix until smooth. Shape into 12 oval patties. Beat remaining 1 egg. Dip patties in egg and then in crumbs, coating well. Heat remaining 2 tablespoons oil in a frying pan. Fry patties over low heat until well browned, about 10 minutes on each side, turning only once. Add more oil, if needed.

Planked Veal Steak

Makes 4 to 6 servings.

    1½ pounds ground stewing veal
    1 egg, lightly beaten
    1 to 2 tablespoons dry onion soup mix
    1 cup soft bread crumbs
    1 cup chicken broth
    2 tablespoons catsup
    2 drops Tabasco sauce
    1 tablespoon butter or margarine, melted
    2 cups mashed potatoes

Combine all ingredients, except butter and potatoes; blend thoroughly. Shape into a 1-inch steak on a greased plank or ovenproof platter. Brush top with melted butter. Bake at 350° for 20 minutes. Surround outer edge of steak with an attractive border of potatoes. Increase oven temperature to 375°. Bake until potatoes are golden brown. Garnish with green peas, if desired.

Keep hands clean when making meat loaf by placing the ingredients in a plastic bag. Mix the meat loaf by pressing on the bag.

Pasta Stuffed with Veal

Makes 6 to 8 servings.

    ½ cup chopped onion
    1 clove garlic, minced
    2 tablespoons olive oil
    1 cup tomato juice
    1 8-ounce can tomato sauce
    1 1-pound can tomatoes, cut up
    ¼ teaspoon thyme
    ¼ teaspoon marjoram
    ¼ teaspoon oregano
    1 teaspoon Worcestershire sauce
    1 pound ground veal
    ¼ cup milk
    1 egg, lightly beaten
    ½ onion, chopped
    1 teaspoon salt
    ¼ teaspoon black pepper
    4 ounces manicotti

Sauté onion and garlic in oil. Add next 7 ingredients and bring to a boil. Reduce heat and simmer for 30 minutes. Combine veal, milk, egg, onion, salt, and pepper; mix well. Stuff uncooked manicotti shells with veal mixture. Pour half of the tomato sauce into an oblong baking dish. Arrange shells in dish. Pour remaining sauce over top. Cover and bake at 375° for 60 minutes.

Veal and Peppers

Makes 4 servings.

- 4 tablespoons butter or margarine
- 1 medium green pepper, cut in ½-inch strips
- 1 medium red pepper, cut in ½-inch strips
- 1 tablespoon vegetable oil
- 1 pound veal, coarsely ground
- 2 tablespoons flour
- 1 tablespoon onion soup mix
- 1 cup water
- 2 tablespoons chili sauce

Heat 2 tablespoons of the butter in a frying pan. Sauté peppers until tender-crisp. Remove from frying pan. Heat the remaining 2 tablespoons butter and the oil. Quickly brown veal. Sprinkle on flour. Add onion soup mix, water, and chili sauce. Cook until thick and bubbly. Stir peppers into mixture. Serve with noodles or rice.

Spaghetti Marinara

Makes 4 servings.

- 1 can anchovy fillets, minced, reserve oil
- 1 onion, minced
- 1 clove garlic, crushed
- ½ pound ground veal
- 1 1-pound can tomatoes
- ½ teaspoon basil
- ½ teaspoon thyme
- 1 pound spaghetti, cooked per package directions and drained
- ½ cup grated Romano cheese
- ½ cup minced parsley

Heat reserved anchovy oil in a saucepan. Sauté onion, garlic, and veal in oil. Add tomatoes, basil, and thyme. Simmer for 20 minutes. Add anchovies. Serve over spaghetti. Garnish with cheese and parsley.

Quick Veal Parmigiana

Makes 4 servings.

- 1 pound ground veal
- 1 egg, lightly beaten
- 1 cup dry bread crumbs
- 3 tablespoons vegetable oil
- 2 cups canned spaghetti sauce with mushrooms
- 4 slices mozzarella cheese

Combine veal and egg; mix thoroughly. Shape into 4 flat patties. Coat both sides with bread crumbs. Heat oil in a frying pan. Brown on both sides. Reduce heat. Add sauce. Top each pattie with cheese. Cover and simmer for 5 to 10 minutes, until cheese melts. Serve with buttered pasta.

Veal Patties with Apples

Makes 4 to 6 servings.

- 1½ pounds ground veal
- 1 egg, lightly beaten
- ½ teaspoon salt
  Dash black pepper
- ½ teaspoon nutmeg
- ½ cup bread crumbs
- 2 tablespoons butter
- 2 tablespoons vegetable oil
- ¼ pound mushrooms, sliced
- 2 apples, unpeeled, sliced
- ⅓ cup brandy
- ½ to ¾ cup cream

Combine veal, egg, seasonings, and bread crumbs; mix well. Form into 6 to 8 patties. Melt butter and oil in a frying pan. Brown patties. Remove from pan and keep warm. Add mushrooms and apples to frying pan. Sauté for 3 to 4 minutes. Pour brandy over mushrooms and apples. Ignite with a match. Shake pan until flames go out. Return veal to pan. Add cream and heat to steaming. Serve over rice.

Baked Veal Patties

Makes 4 servings.

- 1 pound ground stewing veal
- 1 egg, lightly beaten
- 1 cup soft bread crumbs
- 2 tablespoons catsup
- 1 teaspoon mustard
- 1 clove garlic, minced
- 1 tablespoon snipped parsley
- ½ carrot, grated
- 1 small green pepper, minced
- 1 small red pepper or 1 canned pimiento, minced
- ½ cup chicken broth
  Salt and pepper to taste
- 1 tablespoon vegetable oil

Combine all ingredients except oil; mix well. Shape mixture into 4 large patties. Heat oil in a baking dish. Place patties in dish. Bake in a 325° oven for 30 minutes. Do not turn patties over.

Chicken and Turkey

Chicken au Gratin

Makes 8 to 10 servings.

- 1 8-ounce package thin spaghetti, prepared according to package directions and drained
- 2 cups ground, cooked chicken
- 1 small onion, minced
- 1 4-ounce can sliced mushrooms, drained
- 1 10¾-ounce can cream of tomato soup
- 1 cup milk
- ¼ teaspoon black pepper
- 2 cups grated Cheddar cheese
- ½ cup cracker crumbs

Place cooked spaghetti in a 9 x 13-inch baking dish. Sprinkle chicken on top. Combine onion, mushrooms, soup, milk, pepper, and cheese; blend thoroughly. Pour over spaghetti. Sprinkle with crumbs and bake at 350° for 30 minutes until hot and bubbly.

Curried Chicken Pies

Makes 8 pies.

Pastry

- ½ cup cold butter or margarine
- 1 cup flour
  Dash salt
- ½ cup sour half-and-half

Cream butter with an electric mixer. Cut in flour and salt with a fork or pastry blender. Add sour half-and-half; blend thoroughly. Divide dough into 8 equal portions. Roll each into a ball. Wrap and chill for at least 1 hour before using. Roll out dough into circles on a floured board. Divide the Filling equally among the circles. Fold over and seal edges with a fork. Bake at 350° for 25 to 30 minutes until golden brown.

Filling

- 2 tablespoons butter or margarine
- ½ small onion, minced
- ½ rib celery, minced
- ¼ green pepper, minced
- 2 tablespoons minced parsley
- 1 teaspoon curry powder
- 2 cups ground, cooked chicken or turkey
- 1 tablespoon raisins
- 1 tablespoon sherry

Melt butter in a large frying pan. Sauté onion, celery, green pepper, parsley, and curry powder until vegetables are tender-crisp. Add chicken, raisins, and sherry. Simmer for 3 to 4 minutes to blend flavors. Cool.

Chicken Salad in Tomato Shells

Makes 6 servings.

- 6 tomatoes
- 2 cups minced, cooked chicken
- ½ cup minced celery
- ½ cup mayonnaise
- 1 tablespoon olive oil
- 1 teaspoon sherry
- ½ teaspoon sugar
- 1 tablespoon lemon juice
  Lettuce leaves
  Sliced ripe olives
  Parsley sprigs

Remove tops from tomatoes. Scoop out pulp and seeds. Combine chicken, celery, and seasonings. Place tomato shells on lettuce leaves. Lightly spoon salad into shells. Garnish with olives and parsley.

Turkey Meatballs and Spaghetti

Makes 6 servings.

- 1 pound ground turkey
- ½ cup dry bread crumbs
- ¼ cup grated Parmesan cheese
- ¼ cup milk
- ¼ cup minced parsley
- 1 egg
- 1 clove garlic, minced
- ½ teaspoon salt
- ¼ teaspoon black pepper
- 2 cups canned spaghetti sauce
- 1 teaspoon crushed oregano or basil
- 1 pound spaghetti, prepared according to package directions and drained

Combine turkey, crumbs, cheese, milk, parsley, egg, garlic, salt, and pepper in a large bowl; mix well. Shape into meatballs. Bring spaghetti sauce and oregano to a boil in a large saucepan. Add meatballs. Reduce heat and simmer for 20 minutes, carefully turning meatballs to cook through. Serve with hot cooked spaghetti. Pass additional grated Parmesan cheese.

Chicken Salad in Tomato Shells, above

Turkey Enchilada

Makes 6 servings.

- 1 tablespoon vegetable oil
- 1 pound uncooked, ground turkey
- 1 large onion, chopped
- 1 4-ounce can mild or hot green chilies, chopped and drained
- 1 teaspoon salt
- ½ teaspoon ground cumin
- 2 cups sour cream
- 1 10-ounce can enchilada sauce
- 12 frozen flour tortillas, thawed
- 8 ounces sharp Cheddar cheese, grated

Heat oil in a frying pan. Add turkey and onion and sauté 4 to 5 minutes, stirring until turkey is no longer red. Remove from heat. Stir in chilies, salt, cumin, and sour cream. Heat enchilada sauce in a saucepan. Dip 4 of the tortillas in the sauce; place in a 9 x 13-inch baking dish. Spread half of the turkey mixture over the tortillas. Sprinkle on ⅓ of the cheese. Repeat with 4 more tortillas, the remaining turkey mixture, and half of the remaining cheese. Cover with remaining tortillas. Pour remaining enchilada sauce over tortillas. Sprinkle on the remaining cheese. Cover and bake for 35 to 45 minutes or until casserole is bubbly. Let stand 10 minutes before serving.

Turkey Rolls

Makes 14 to 16 rolls.

- 3½ to 4 pounds turkey thighs, frozen or fresh, skinned and meat removed from bones
- 2 eggs, lightly beaten
- 2 large potatoes, coarsely shredded
- 6 carrots, coarsely shredded
- 1 small onion, chopped
- ½ cup chopped green pepper
- 1 clove garlic, minced
- 2 tablespoons lemon juice
- ½ teaspoon crushed thyme
- 2 teaspoons salt
  Freshly ground black pepper
  Vegetable oil

Grind turkey meat in a meat grinder or food processor; repeat. Place turkey in a mixing bowl. Add eggs and blend thoroughly. Add remaining ingredients, except vegetable oil, and blend thoroughly. Shape into 4 x 2½-inch rolls. Arrange on a greased baking sheet. Bake at 400° for 45 minutes. Brush with vegetable oil halfway through the baking time.

Turkey-Barley Casserole

Makes 4 servings.

- 1 small onion, chopped
- 1 rib celery, chopped
- ½ green pepper, chopped
- 1 tablespoon margarine or butter
- 3 tablespoons vegetable oil, divided
- ¾ cup barley
- 1¾ cups beef broth
- 1 1½-pound turkey thigh, frozen or fresh, skinned and meat removed from bone
- 1 tablespoon paprika
- 1 teaspoon Worcestershire sauce
  Salt and pepper to taste
- 1 to 2 cups boiling water
- 1 10-ounce package frozen green peas

Sauté onion, celery, and green pepper in the margarine and 1 tablespoon of the oil until slightly soft. Add barley and stir for 3 to 4 minutes. Add beef broth. Bring to a boil. Cover, reduce heat, and simmer 15 minutes. Grind turkey in a meat grinder or food processor. Sauté turkey in the remaining 2 tablespoons oil until it is no longer red, stirring to break it up. Add cooked turkey to barley-vegetable mixture. Add remaining ingredients, except peas, and enough boiling water so that mixture is very loose. Stir to blend thoroughly, cover and simmer 30 minutes or until barley is tender, stirring once or twice. Add peas and cook 5 minutes. Serve in a heated casserole.

Chinese Turkey and Noodles

Makes 4 servings.

- 1 tablespoon vegetable oil
- 1 pound ground turkey
- 1 clove garlic, minced
- 3 to 4 green onions, sliced
- 2 tablespoons dry sherry
- 3 tablespoons soy sauce
- ½ cup chili sauce or catsup
- ¼ cup water
- 1 tablespoon vinegar
- ½ pound very thin noodles, cooked and drained
- 2 green onions, cut into strips

Heat oil in a large frying pan. Stir-fry turkey, garlic, and onions, breaking up meat with a spoon. Stir in remaining ingredients, except noodles and green onions. Bring to a boil. Reduce heat and simmer 5 to 10 minutes until liquid is reduced. Arrange noodles on a platter. Spoon sauce over top. Garnish with green onion strips.

Turkey-Eggplant Casserole

Makes 4 to 6 servings.

- 1 pound ground turkey
- 1 onion, chopped
- 1 clove garlic, minced
- ¼ cup snipped parsley
- 1 teaspoon salt
- ¼ teaspoon black pepper
- 1 ¾-pound medium eggplant, unpeeled, cut into ½-inch cubes
- 1 teaspoon crushed oregano
- 1 8-ounce can tomato sauce
- 4 ounces sharp Cheddar cheese, grated

Mix turkey, onion, garlic, parsley, salt, and pepper lightly with a fork. Grease a 1½-quart casserole. Spread a third of the eggplant over the bottom. Spread half of the turkey mixture on top. Spread with a third of the eggplant, the remaining turkey and eggplant. Stir oregano into tomato sauce. Pour over eggplant. Cover and bake in 375° oven for 45 minutes. Uncover. Sprinkle on cheese. Bake for 15 minutes until cheese is melted. Let stand 10 minutes before serving.

Turkey Burgers

Makes 4 servings.

- 1 egg, lightly beaten
- 2 tablespoons grated onion
- 1 teaspoon garlic powder
- 2 tablespoons tomato paste
- ¼ cup wheat germ
- 1 teaspoon salt
- ¼ teaspoon black pepper
- 3 cups ground, uncooked turkey (ground twice)
- 1 tablespoon vegetable oil
- 2 tablespoons margarine or butter
- 1 4-ounce can mushrooms, drained
- 1 tablespoon flour
- 1 cup milk or cream
  Pinch salt, nutmeg, pepper
- 2 tablespoons snipped parsley
- 1 tablespoon sherry

Combine egg, onion, garlic powder, tomato paste, wheat germ, salt, and pepper; mix well. Add the ground turkey; mix thoroughly. Form into 4 patties. Heat the oil and 1 tablespoon of the margarine in a frying pan. Brown patties well on 1 side. Turn and brown the other side. Reduce heat to low. Cover and cook 5 minutes or until turkey is no longer pink. Remove from pan and keep warm. To the pan add remaining 1 tablespoon margarine and mushrooms. Sprinkle in flour; mix well. Add 1 cup milk; cook and stir until thickened. Add a pinch of salt, nutmeg, pepper, parsley, and sherry. Cook 3 to 4 minutes, stirring frequently. Pour over burgers.

Turkey-Rice Casserole

Makes 4 servings.

- 1 tablespoon vegetable oil
- ½ pound ground turkey
- 1 cup chopped onion
- 1 clove garlic, minced
- 1 cup raw, long grain rice
- 1 28-ounce can whole, peeled tomatoes, drained; reserve liquid
- 1 teaspoon chicken bouillon granules
- 1 teaspoon crushed oregano
- ½ teaspoon salt
- ¼ teaspoon black pepper
- 1 cup chopped green pepper
- 2 ounces cubed mozzarella cheese

Heat oil in a frying pan. Sauté turkey, onion, and garlic until turkey is no longer pink. Stir in rice and cook for 2 minutes. Add enough water to tomato liquid to make 1½ cups. Stir in rice mixture. Add bouillon and seasonings. Bring just to a boil; cover frying pan and simmer for 10 minutes. Add green pepper and tomatoes; simmer 10 minutes or until rice is tender. Sprinkle on cheese. Cover pan and remove from heat. Let stand for 1 to 2 minutes, until cheese melts.

Turkey Quiche

Makes 4 to 6 servings.

- 1 tablespoon vegetable oil
- ½ pound ground turkey
- ½ small onion, chopped
- 1 9-inch unbaked piecrust or buttered 1½-quart rectangular baking dish
- 1 cup shredded Cheddar or Swiss cheese
- 4 eggs
- 1½ cups milk
- ½ teaspoon salt
- ¼ teaspoon black pepper
  Dash ground nutmeg

Heat oil in a small saucepan. Sauté turkey and onion for 3 to 4 minutes or until turkey is no longer red. Spoon mixture into piecrust or buttered baking dish. Sprinkle on cheese. Beat eggs, milk, and seasonings together; pour over turkey. Bake at 350° for 35 minutes or until a knife inserted in the center comes out clean. Let stand 10 minutes before serving.

Ham

Stuffed Eggs

Makes 24 stuffed eggs.

12 hard-cooked eggs
½ cup ground, cooked ham
½ cup mayonnaise
¼ cup sour half-and-half
1 teaspoon curry powder
½ teaspoon salt
  Dash Tabasco sauce

Carefully slice eggs in half lengthwise; remove yolks. Crumble yolks; mix in remaining ingredients. Use a spoon or pastry tube to fill egg whites. Chill thoroughly before serving.

Ham and Pineapple Salad

Makes 4 to 6 servings.

2 cups ground, cooked ham
½ cup mayonnaise
1 tablespoon prepared horseradish
1 tablespoon prepared mustard
  Lettuce leaves
1 13-ounce can pineapple chunks, drained
1 green pepper, cut into strips

Combine ham, mayonnaise, horseradish, and mustard. Line a platter with lettuce leaves. Mound ham salad in center. Garnish platter with pineapple chunks and green pepper strips. Serve with hot biscuits.

Ham Mousse

Makes 10 to 12 servings.

1 tablespoon unflavored gelatin
¼ cup cold water
1½ cups boiling chicken stock
3 cups ground, cooked ham
¼ cup minced celery
½ small onion, minced
¼ cup minced sweet pickle or relish
⅓ cup mayonnaise
2 tablespoons sour half-and-half
2 tablespoons catsup

Soften gelatin in the cold water. Add gelatin to chicken stock; stir until dissolved. Chill until nearly set. Stir in remaining ingredients until well-blended. Pour into an oiled, 6-cup ring mold. Chill until firm. Unmold onto lettuce or endive. Fill the center with chicken salad and garnish with fresh fruit, if desired.

Pineapple-Topped Ham

Makes 8 servings.

2 cups ground, cooked ham
1 egg, lightly beaten
2 tablespoons peanut butter
1 tablespoon mayonnaise
16 slices pineapple
¼ cup butter or margarine
⅓ cup packed brown sugar

Combine ham, egg, peanut butter, and mayonnaise; blend thoroughly. Place 8 slices of pineapple on broiler pan. Top with ¼ cup of the ham mixture and another slice of pineapple. Broil 3 to 4 inches from heat for about 5 minutes. Turn. Top with butter and brown sugar. Broil for about 5 minutes or until bubbly.

Ham Ring

Makes 4 to 6 servings.

2½ cups ground, cooked ham
¾ pound ground, raw pork
2 cups crushed wheat flakes cereal
2 eggs, lightly beaten
½ cup milk
1 tablespoon prepared mustard
1 onion, minced

Combine all ingredients; mix well. Pack into a greased, 6-cup ring mold or loaf pan. Bake at 350° for 50 to 60 minutes. Serve with Mustard Sauce.

Mustard Sauce

Dissolve equal parts of prepared mustard and currant jelly. Heat through.

Grilled Ham Sandwiches

Makes 4 servings.

2 cups cooked, ground ham
¼ cup sweet pickle relish
⅓ cup mayonnaise
8 slices bread
4 slices American or Swiss cheese
2 tablespoons butter or margarine, softened

Combine ham, relish, and mayonnaise. Divide among 4 slices of bread; spread. Top with 1 slice of cheese and remaining bread. Spread outside of sandwiches with butter. Heat a frying pan. Grill sandwiches on both sides until brown.

Ham Mousse, above

Ham Pasties

Makes 6 pasties.

- 1 tablespoon flour
- 1 teaspoon sugar
- ¼ teaspoon allspice
- ¼ teaspoon cinnamon
- ½ cup mayonnaise
- ½ cup sour half-and-half
- 3 cups ground cooked ham
- 3 apples, diced
- ½ cup raisins
- 2 tablespoons snipped parsley
- 2 crust piecrust mix, prepared according to directions, divided into 6 equal portions and chilled slightly

Combine all ingredients, except crust; blend thoroughly. Roll each ball of dough into a 7-inch circle. Spoon ½ cup of the ham mixture down the center of each circle. Moisten edges of dough slightly with water. Fold dough over filling; press to seal. Place on an ungreased baking sheet. Bake at 400° for 35 to 40 minutes until golden brown. Serve hot or cold with additional half-and-half.

Ham Cakes

Makes 6 servings.

- 2 cups ground, cooked ham (about 1 pound)
- 2 tablespoons minced onion
- ½ cup fine bread or cracker crumbs
- 2 eggs, lightly beaten
- 1 tablespoon snipped parsley
- 1 teaspoon dry mustard
- 1 tablespoon vegetable oil
- ½ cup water
- 1 cup sour cream

Combine ham, onion, crumbs, eggs, parsley, and mustard; mix well. Shape into 6 cakes. Heat oil in a frying pan. Brown cakes on both sides. Remove to a warm platter. Pour water into frying pan; bring to a boil. Reduce heat. Add sour cream and heat through. Do not boil. Spoon over ham cakes.

Ham and Potato Cakes

Makes 4 to 6 cakes.

- 2 cups mashed potatoes
- 2 cups ground, cooked ham
- 1 small onion, minced
- 1 egg, lightly beaten
- 2 tablespoons snipped parsley
- ½ teaspoon marjoram
- 1 cup cracker crumbs
- 2 to 4 tablespoons butter or margarine

Combine potatoes, ham, onion, egg, parsley, and marjoram; mix well. Shape into 4 to 6 cakes. Roll in cracker crumbs. Melt butter in a frying pan. Brown cakes in butter. Serve with scrambled eggs and broiled tomatoes.

Ham and Egg Roll

Makes 8 to 10 servings.

- 1 8-ounce package cream cheese, softened
- 2 tablespoons milk
- 2 cups ground, cooked ham
- 8 to 10 pitted ripe olives, sliced
- 4 hard-cooked eggs, chopped
- ½ teaspoon marjoram
- ½ teaspoon salt
- ½ teaspoon black pepper
- 1 Recipe for Pastry on page 38
- 1 egg yolk, lightly beaten

Combine cream cheese and milk; mix well. Add ham, olives, eggs, and seasonings. Roll out Pastry into a 16-inch square. Spoon ham filling onto pastry 3 inches from one edge, and 2 inches from each end (making a 12 x 13-inch strip). Fold ends in over filling. Roll up jelly-roll fashion from the end nearest the filling. Place on a greased baking sheet. Brush with egg yolk. Bake at 350° for 35 to 45 minutes or until golden brown.

Ham and Cheese Tacos

Makes 16 tacos.

- 1 cup chopped onion
- 1 cup chopped celery
- 3 tablespoons butter or margarine
- 1 pound ground, cooked ham
- 1 16-ounce can tomatoes, chopped, reserve liquid
- 1 6-ounce can tomato paste
- ½ teaspoon sugar
- ½ teaspoon chili powder
  Dash Tabasco sauce
- ½ pound American cheese, cut into 16 sticks
- 16 taco shells
  Shredded lettuce

Sauté onion and celery in butter until just tender. Add ham, tomatoes with liquid, tomato paste, sugar, chili powder, and Tabasco. Simmer uncovered for 30 minutes, stirring frequently. Place a cheese stick in a taco shell. Spoon in ¼ cup of the tomato-meat mixture. Top each with shredded lettuce.

Ham Burgers

Makes 4 servings.

- 1 pound ground, cooked ham
- 1 small onion, minced
- 1 3-ounce package cream cheese, softened
- 1 tablespoon mayonnaise
- 2 tablespoons prepared mustard
- 4 slices tomato
- 4 slices Swiss cheese
- 4 rye rolls, split and toasted

Combine ham, onion, cream cheese, mayonnaise, and mustard; mix well. Shape into 4 patties. Place on a broiler pan. Broil for 3 to 4 minutes; turn. Top with a slice of tomato and a slice of cheese. Broil until cheese is bubbly. Serve on toasted rye rolls.

Ham Baskets

Makes 12 servings.

- 2 tablespoons butter
- ½ pound mushrooms, sliced
- 3 cups ground, cooked ham
- 1 10-ounce package peas, thawed and drained
- 2 tablespoons flour
- 2 tablespoons sherry
- ¾ cup milk
- 2 tablespoons snipped chives
- 2 tablespoons minced pimiento
- 12 patty shells, baked

Melt butter in a saucepan. Sauté mushrooms until tender. Add ham and peas and cook for 3 to 4 minutes. Sprinkle on flour; stir to blend. Gradually add sherry and milk; cook until slightly thickened, stirring constantly. Add chives and pimiento. Heat to steaming. Spoon into baked patty shells.

Ham Patties

Makes 6 servings.

- 2 cups ground, cooked ham (about 1 pound)
- 2 tablespoons minced onion
- ½ cup bread or cracker crumbs
- 2 eggs, lightly beaten
- 1 tablespoon snipped parsley
- 1 teaspoon dry mustard
  Salt and pepper to taste
- 1 tablespoon vegetable oil
- ½ teaspoon paprika
- ½ cup water
- 1 cup sour cream

Combine ham, onion, cracker crumbs, eggs, parsley, mustard, salt, and pepper; mix well.

Shape into 6 patties. Heat oil in a frying pan. Brown patties on both sides. Place on a serving platter. Add paprika and water to pan; bring to a boil. Reduce heat and stir in sour cream; heat through. Spoon over patties.

Quick Jambalaya

Makes 6 servings.

- 2 tablespoons butter or margarine
- 1 rib celery, chopped
- 1 onion, chopped
- 1 green pepper, chopped
- 1 clove garlic, minced
- 1 cup uncooked, long grain rice
- 1½ cups chicken broth
- 1 16-ounce can tomatoes, cut up
- 3 to 4 dashes Tabasco sauce
- 2 cups ground, cooked ham
- ½ 10-ounce package frozen peas, optional

Heat butter in a saucepan. Sauté celery, onion, green pepper, and garlic until tender but not brown. Stir in remaining ingredients, except peas; bring to a boil. Reduce heat, cover, and simmer for 20 minutes or until rice is tender and liquid is absorbed. Stir in peas, if desired. Heat until just tender. Serve with cornbread and coleslaw.

Ham-Filled Omelet

Makes 2 servings.

- 4 eggs at room temperature
- 2 tablespoons milk or water at room temperature
- 1 tablespoon butter or vegetable oil

Combine eggs and milk; mix until lightly blended. Slowly heat butter or oil in an 8-inch frying or omelet pan until bubbly hot. Pour eggs into pan. As edges set, loosen edges a little at a time to allow uncooked portion to run underneath. When omelet is firm to the touch and dry looking, spoon on filling. Fold omelet in half with a spatula. Turn onto a heated platter. Serve immediately.

Fillings

- ½ to ¾ pound ground, cooked ham

Combine ham with 1 or more of the following:

- ½ cup grated cheese
- 1 small onion, minced and sautéed
- 4 to 5 mushrooms, sliced and sautéed
- ½ green pepper, diced and sautéed
- 1 tomato, peeled and diced

Ham-on-Rye Casserole

Makes 6 to 8 servings.

2 cups rye bread cubes
1 cup grated Monterey Jack cheese
6 eggs, lightly beaten
2 cups milk
½ teaspoon salt
1 teaspoon dry mustard
½ onion, minced
¼ cup snipped parsley
¼ teaspoon black pepper
1 cup ground, cooked ham

Lightly oil a 9 x 13-inch casserole. Spread bread cubes and cheese over bottom. Mix eggs, milk, and seasonings. Pour over bread and cheese. Sprinkle on ham. Bake at 325° for 40 minutes or until eggs are set.

Ham and Cheese Puff

Makes 6 servings.

12 slices bread, each cut into 4 strips
1 cup ground, cooked ham
1 cup shredded Monterey Jack or Cheddar cheese
4 eggs, lightly beaten
2½ cups milk
2 tablespoons prepared mustard
1 teaspoon salt
Dash Tabasco sauce

Arrange half of the bread strips in a lightly greased casserole. Sprinkle on ham and cheese. Cover with remaining bread strips. Combine eggs, milk, mustard, salt, and Tabasco; beat with a wire whisk or fork to mix thoroughly. Pour over all. Let stand for 30 minutes. Bake at 350° for 30 to 45 minutes or until puffy and golden. Let stand 10 minutes before serving.

Glazed Ham Balls

Makes 8 servings.

4 cups ground, cooked ham
⅓ cup fine cracker crumbs
1 egg, lightly beaten
⅔ cup evaporated milk
Dash Tabasco sauce
Pinch thyme
1 tablespoon vinegar
2 tablespoons brown sugar
½ teaspoon dry mustard
1½ teaspoons flour

Combine ham, crumbs, egg, milk, Tabasco, and thyme; blend thoroughly. Shape into 8 balls. Place in a baking dish or pan. Bake at 350° for 20 minutes. Combine remaining ingredients in a nonstick pan; bring to a boil. Stir and cook for 30 seconds. Remove from heat. Drain fat from meat. Brush glaze over meatballs. Broil about 8 inches from heat source for 2 minutes. Baste with juices. Serve with macaroni and cheese.

Ham and Cheese Pie

Makes 8 servings.

1 double piecrust; pat into bottom and sides of a 9 x 13-inch baking pan
3 tablespoons butter
3 cups cooked, ground ham
½ pound mushrooms, sliced
3 onions, sliced
2 eggs, lightly beaten
½ cup milk
½ pound Swiss cheese, grated
2 tomatoes, sliced
1 cup soft bread crumbs

Melt butter in a saucepan. Add ham, mushrooms, and onions; sauté until onions are tender. Cool. Mix eggs and milk together. Add ham mixture and half of the cheese; mix lightly. Pour into piecrust. Top with sliced tomatoes and remaining cheese mixed with crumbs. Bake at 350° for 30 to 35 minutes until hot and bubbly.

Baked Stuffed Squash

Makes 6 servings.

3 acorn squash
½ cup brown sugar
1 teaspoon cinnamon
6 teaspoons butter
1 pound ground, cooked ham or turkey ham
1 onion, minced
½ cup soft bread crumbs
1 cup applesauce

Bake squash at 350° for 45 minutes to 1 hour, until soft to the touch. (Can also be tested with a fork.) Cut in half lengthwise; remove seeds. Sprinkle sugar, cinnamon, and 1 teaspoon butter in each half. Mash lightly with a fork. Combine ham, onion, bread crumbs, and applesauce; blend thoroughly. Spoon into squash halves. Bake at 350° for 20 minutes or until crispy and hot.

Ham and Noodles

Makes 6 to 8 servings.

    5 tablespoons butter or margarine
    1 rib celery, chopped
    2 green onions, chopped
    ¼ cup flour
    1 teaspoon salt
    ¼ teaspoon black pepper
    3 cups milk
    1 3-ounce package cream cheese
    ¼ cup dry bread crumbs
    1 8-ounce package thin noodles, cooked according
      to package directions and drained
    2 cups ground, cooked ham
    1 10-ounce package frozen, chopped broccoli,
      thawed

Melt 4 tablespoons of the butter in a saucepan. Sauté celery and onions until tender. Stir in flour, salt, and pepper until blended. Gradually stir in milk. Cook slowly until sauce is thickened, stirring constantly. Add cream cheese and stir until melted. Melt remaining 1 tablespoon butter. Stir into bread crumbs. Stir cheese sauce into noodles and ham. Place broccoli in a 9 x 12-inch baking dish. Place noodles and ham over broccoli. Sprinkle on buttered crumbs. Bake at 350° for 30 to 35 minutes, until hot and bubbly.

Spaghetti Carbonara

Makes 2 servings.

    ½ pound spaghetti, cooked according to package
      directions and drained
    4 tablespoons butter
    1 cup light cream
    ½ pound ground, cooked ham
    2 eggs, lightly beaten
    ½ cup grated Parmesan cheese

Melt butter in a saucepan. Add cream. Heat to steaming. Stir in ham. Stir the ham mixture into the eggs a little at a time; blend thoroughly. Return to heat. Add cheese; heat to steaming. Serve over cooked spaghetti.

Ham Casserole

Makes 4 to 6 servings.

    ½ teaspoon cinnamon
    ¼ cup brown sugar
    2 tart apples, peeled and sliced
    2 cups cooked and mashed rutabaga
    1½ cups ground, cooked ham
    3 slices American cheese, cut into strips

Combine cinnamon and brown sugar; mix lightly. Toss apple slices in cinnamon and brown sugar mixture. Place half of the rutabaga in a greased casserole; smooth. Top with half of the apples, the ham, remaining rutabaga, and remaining apples. Bake at 350° for 40 minutes. Place strips of cheese on top. Bake for 10 minutes until cheese melts.

Ham and Mushroom Pizza

Makes 4 servings.

    1 12 to 14-inch pizza crust
    2 tablespoons butter or margarine
    ½ pound mushrooms, sliced
    1 onion, minced
    1 cup ground, cooked ham
    1 cup grated Parmesan cheese
    1 8-ounce can tomato sauce
    1 teaspoon oregano

Preheat oven to 425°. Melt butter in a small frying pan. Sauté mushrooms and onion until tender-crisp. Sprinkle mushrooms, onion, ham, and cheese over crust. Pour on tomato sauce. Sprinkle on oregano. Bake for 30 minutes until crisp and golden.

Sweet-Sour Ham Patties

Makes 4 to 6 servings.

    1 tablespoon butter or margarine
    1 onion, minced
    ½ cup red wine
    2 cloves
    1 bay leaf
    1 pound ground, cooked ham
    1 egg
    ¼ cup dry bread crumbs
    ¼ cup raisins
    1 slice bacon, cut into small pieces
    1 small head red cabbage, chopped
    2 tart apples, chopped
    2 tablespoons currant jelly

Melt butter in a frying pan. Sauté onion until tender. Add wine, cloves, and bay leaf; simmer for 5 minutes. In a bowl, combine ham, egg, bread crumbs, and raisins. Shape into 6 to 8 patties. Add to wine sauce and simmer for 5 minutes. Fry bacon in a large frying pan. Add cabbage and apples. Cover and simmer for 20 minutes or until cabbage is tender. Add ham patties and sauce; simmer for 15 to 20 minutes, uncovered. Just before serving stir in currant jelly.

Eggplant and Ham

Makes 6 to 8 servings.

 1 tablespoon butter
 1 tablespoon vegetable oil
 1 cup minced onion
 1 clove garlic, minced
 ½ pound fresh mushrooms, chopped
   Juice of 1 lemon
   Salt and pepper to taste
 3 tablespoons snipped parsley
 1 teaspoon basil
 ½ pound ham, coarsely ground
 ½ cup bread crumbs
 ½ cup grated Parmesan cheese
 2 eggplants, sliced ½ inch thick
   Flour
 1 cup vegetable oil
 2 tomatoes, sliced

Heat butter and oil in a frying pan. Sauté onion and garlic until tender. Add mushrooms, lemon juice, salt, pepper, parsley, and basil. Cook over high heat, stirring until liquid evaporates. Add ham and cook 5 minutes, stirring frequently. Stir in ¼ cup of the bread crumbs and ¼ cup of the Parmesan cheese; remove from heat. Dust eggplant slices with flour. Heat oil in a large frying pan. Brown eggplant on both sides. Drain on paper toweling. Arrange 1 layer of eggplant in a baking dish. Spoon filling on top almost to edges, mounding it in the center. Cover with overlapping slices of remaining eggplant. Arrange tomato slices on top. Combine remaining bread crumbs and Parmesan cheese. Sprinkle over top. Bake at 400° for 35 to 45 minutes. Remove from oven, drain liquid, and cool for 5 minutes.

Meat and Potato Pie

Makes 6 servings.

 3 cups ground, cooked ham
 1 egg, lightly beaten
 1 cup milk
 1 cup dry bread crumbs
 ½ small onion, minced
 1 tablespoon Worcestershire sauce
 2 cups mashed sweet potatoes
 ¼ cup packed brown sugar
 ¼ cup butter

Combine ham, egg, milk, bread crumbs, onion, and Worcestershire sauce; blend thoroughly. Pat into a pie plate. Spread mashed sweet potatoes on top. Sprinkle on brown sugar. Dot with butter. Bake for 30 minutes or until bubbly.

Hawaiian Ham and Pineapple Pie

Makes 6 servings.

 1 unbaked, 9-inch pie shell
 1 pound ground, cooked ham
 ⅓ cup dry bread crumbs
 2 eggs, lightly beaten
 ½ cup milk
 2 tablespoons snipped green onions
   Pinch ground cloves
 1 tablespoon mustard
1½ cups crushed pineapple, drained
 ¼ cup packed brown sugar

Combine ham, crumbs, eggs, milk, onion, cloves, mustard, and ½ cup pineapple; mix lightly. Spoon into pie shell; smooth top. Combine remaining 1 cup pineapple and brown sugar. Arrange attractively on top of ham mixture. Bake at 350° for 45 minutes.

Stuffed Pepper Salad

Makes 8 shells.

 2 cups ground, cooked ham
 ½ cup cream-style cottage cheese
 ½ cup mayonnaise
 1 small onion, minced
 2 tablespoons sweet pickle relish
 4 large peppers, cut in half lengthwise and seeded
   Cucumber slices
   Lettuce leaves

Combine ham, cottage cheese, mayonnaise, onion, and relish. Spoon into pepper shells. Garnish with cucumber slices. Arrange on lettuce leaves.

Ham a la King

Makes 6 servings.

 3 tablespoons butter or margarine
 2 cups ground, cooked ham
 ½ pound mushrooms, sliced
 ½ green pepper, diced
 ¼ cup flour
 2 cups milk
 2 hard-cooked eggs, diced
 2 tablespoons sherry
 ¼ cup chopped pimiento
 6 waffles or English muffins, split and toasted

Melt butter in a saucepan. Sauté ham, mushrooms, and pepper until tender. Sprinkle on flour and stir. Add milk and cook gently until thickened, stirring constantly. Add eggs, sherry, and pimiento; mix lightly. Serve on waffles or muffins.

Pork

Pork Goulash

Makes 6 to 8 servings.

- 1 pound ground pork
- 1 onion, chopped
- ¼ pound mushrooms, sliced
- 1 tablespoon paprika
- 1 tablespoon Worcestershire sauce
- 1 pound sauerkraut, drained
- ½ cup sour cream

Brown pork, onion, and mushrooms in a large frying pan; drain fat. Add paprika, Worcestershire, and sauerkraut. Cover and simmer for 30 minutes. Just before serving, stir in sour cream. Heat through, but do not boil. Serve over noodles.

Pork Pie

Makes 4 to 6 servings.

- 1 double piecrust recipe, rolled into 2 9-inch crusts
- 1 pound ground pork
- 1 onion, chopped
- 1 rib celery, minced
- 1 carrot, chopped
- 1 clove garlic, crushed
- ½ teaspoon salt
- ½ teaspoon thyme
- ¼ teaspoon ground cloves
- ¾ cup water
- 2 potatoes, peeled and chopped

Sauté pork for 3 to 4 minutes in a large frying pan; drain fat. Add remaining ingredients. Simmer for 30 minutes, stirring occasionally. Remove from heat and cool. Fit one pastry crust into a 9-inch pie plate. Spoon pork mixture into pastry shell. Cover with top crust. Pinch edges together and flute. Pierce top in several places with a fork. Bake at 425° for 25 minutes or until golden brown.

Sausage Cornbake

Makes approximately 14 muffins, 18 sticks, or 1 medium frying panful.

- 1¼ cups milk
- ¼ cup shortening
- 1 egg, lightly beaten
- 2 cups white cornmeal
- 3 teaspoons baking powder
- 1 teaspoon salt
- 1 teaspoon sugar
- ½ pound sausage, cooked and drained

Grease muffin pans, cornstick mold, or heat-proof frying pan. Heat in a 450° oven. Combine milk and shortening with egg; mix lightly. Stir in cornmeal, baking powder, salt, sugar, and sausage; blend well. Pour batter into hot, greased pans. Bake 25 to 30 minutes, until golden. Serve with syrup for breakfast or lunch.

Pork Chow Mein

Makes 6 servings.

- 1 pound lean ground pork
- 2 cups diagonally sliced celery
- ½ onion, chopped
- 1 tablespoon brown sugar
- 1 4-ounce can mushrooms, reserve liquid
- 1 tablespoon flour
- 1 cup milk
- ¼ cup soy sauce
- 1 pound fresh bean sprouts

Sauté pork, celery, and onion until browned; drain fat. Stir in brown sugar and reserved mushroom liquid. Cover and simmer for 20 minutes. Stir in flour. Gradually stir in milk. Simmer until thickened, stirring constantly. Add soy sauce, bean sprouts, and mushrooms. Heat through. Serve with chow mein noodles.

Roast Pork Jardiniere Stew

Makes 6 servings.

- 2 pounds ground roast pork
- 1 cup soft bread crumbs
- 1 cup applesauce
- 1 egg, lightly beaten
- 1 teaspoon salt
- ¼ teaspoon allspice
- ½ cup flour
- 3 tablespoons vegetable oil
- 3 carrots, sliced
- 2 onions, sliced
- 1 green pepper, chopped
- 2 potatoes, diced
- 2 cups chicken broth

Combine pork, bread crumbs, applesauce, egg, salt, and allspice. Shape into meatballs; roll in flour. Heat oil in a frying pan; brown meatballs, a few at a time, on all sides. Remove to casserole. Place vegetables and broth in pan. Bring to a boil and scrape browned bits from bottom of pan. Pour all over meatballs in casserole. Bake at 350° for 30 minutes.

Lasagna Roll

Makes 4 servings.

Meat Filling

- ½ pound Italian sausage, casing removed
- ½ pound ground beef
- ¾ cup chopped onion
- 1 clove garlic, minced
- 1 tablespoon parsley flakes
- ½ teaspoon crushed basil
- ½ teaspoon crushed oregano
- ½ teaspoon salt
- ¼ teaspoon black pepper
- 1 6-ounce can tomato paste

Brown Italian sausage and ground beef in a frying pan; drain fat. Add remaining Meat Filling ingredients. Simmer uncovered for 5 minutes.

Cheese Filling

- 1 cup creamed cottage cheese, slightly drained
- 1 egg
- ¼ cup grated Parmesan cheese

Combine Cheese Filling ingredients; mix thoroughly.

Crust

- 2 8-ounce cans refrigerated quick crescent rolls
- 3 4-inch square slices mozzarella cheese
- 1 egg, lightly beaten

Separate crescent dough into 8 rectangles. Place dough on an ungreased baking sheet, overlapping edges to make a 13 x 15-inch rectangle. Seal at perforations. Spread half of the Meat Filling lengthwise down the center half of the dough to within 1 inch of the 13-inch ends. Spread Cheese Filling over Meat Filling. Spoon remaining Meat Filling over top. Place cheese slices over Meat Filling, overlapping slightly. Fold long sides of dough over filling, overlapping edges ¼ inch. Pinch overlapped edges to seal. Brush with beaten egg. Bake in a preheated 375° oven for 20 to 25 minutes or until deep golden brown. Let stand 10 minutes before slicing.

Sausage-Cheese Soufflé

Makes 6 servings.

- 1 pound bulk pork sausage
- 6 slices white bread, crusts trimmed
- 4 ounces shredded Cheddar or processed Swiss cheese
- 4 eggs, lightly beaten
- 1¾ cups milk
- 1 teaspoon mustard

Brown sausage in a frying pan; drain fat. Place bread in a 12 x 7½-inch baking pan. Sprinkle sausage and cheese on top of bread. Combine eggs, milk, and mustard; blend thoroughly. Pour over cheese. Let stand for 30 minutes. Bake in a preheated 325° oven for 1 hour or until eggs are set.

Sweet-Sour Pork Patties

Makes 4 servings.

- 1 pound ground pork
- ½ cup dry bread crumbs
- 1 egg, lightly beaten
- 2 tablespoons soy sauce
- ½ teaspoon ginger
- ½ teaspoon dry mustard
- 1 tablespoon vegetable oil
- 1 green pepper, cut into chunks
- 3 green onions, sliced
- 1 13-ounce can pineapple chunks, undrained
- 3 tablespoons brown sugar
- 3 tablespoons cornstarch
- 3 tablespoons white vinegar
- 3 tablespoons water

Combine pork, bread crumbs, egg, soy sauce, ginger, and mustard; mix well. Shape into 4 to 6 patties. Heat oil in a large frying pan. Brown patties in oil; drain fat. Add green pepper, onions, and pineapple with juice. Cover and simmer for 20 minutes. Blend together sugar, cornstarch, vinegar, and water. Add to frying pan. Stir until thickened and clear. Serve over rice.

MacSausage Casserole

Makes 4 servings.

- 1 pound bulk pork sausage
- ½ onion, chopped
- 1 cup chopped celery
- 2 8-ounce cans tomato sauce
- ½ teaspoon crushed basil
- 2 cups elbow macaroni, cooked as directed on package
- 8 ounces mozzarella cheese, sliced

Brown sausage in a large frying pan; drain fat. Add onion and celery; sauté until tender. Add tomato sauce and basil. Cover and simmer for 5 minutes. Lightly oil a 1½-quart casserole. Layer half of the macaroni, half of the meat sauce, and half of the cheese in the casserole. Repeat layers, ending with cheese. Bake in a 350° oven for 30 minutes.

Stuffed Eggplant Parmigiana

Makes 4 servings.

- ¾ pound bulk Italian sausage
- 1 1-pound can tomatoes
- 1 6-ounce can tomato paste
- 2 tablespoons chopped parsley
- 1 tablespoon chopped onion
- 1 clove garlic, minced
- ½ teaspoon salt
- ½ teaspoon crushed basil
- 2 medium-size eggplants
- 1 cup shredded mozzarella cheese
- ½ cup grated Parmesan cheese

Brown sausage in a large frying pan; drain on paper toweling. Drain fat from frying pan. Combine sausage, tomatoes, tomato paste, parsley, onion, garlic, salt, and basil in frying pan. Cover and simmer for 15 minutes, stirring occasionally. Cut eggplants in half lengthwise. Scoop out pulp; cut into ½-inch cubes. Reserve shells. Add eggplant to tomato mixture. Cover and simmer about 15 minutes, stirring occasionally. Place eggplant shells in a 9 x 13-inch baking dish. Fill shells with half of the tomato mixture. Sprinkle on mozzarella cheese. Top with remaining tomato mixture. Sprinkle on Parmesan cheese. Bake uncovered at 350° for 30 minutes.

Sausage and Sauerkraut

Makes 6 servings.

- 1 pound bulk pork sausage
- 1 onion, sliced
- 1 1-pound can sauerkraut, drained
- 1 teaspoon brown sugar
- 2 cups mashed potatoes
- 4 tablespoons grated Parmesan cheese

Brown sausage and onion in a large frying pan; drain fat. Place in a 3-quart casserole. Combine sauerkraut and brown sugar. Place sauerkraut on top of sausage. Spread potatoes over top. Sprinkle on cheese. Bake at 350° for 35 to 40 minutes.

Sausage Quiche

Makes 6 servings.

- ½ pound bulk pork sausage
- 1 9-inch pie shell, baked at 350° for 7 minutes
- 4 eggs, lightly beaten
- 1 cup milk
- 4 ounces Swiss cheese, grated

Brown sausage in a frying pan; drain fat. Spread sausage over the bottom of the pie shell. Combine eggs, milk, and cheese; blend thoroughly. Pour over sausage. Bake at 350° for 30 to 35 minutes or until eggs are set. Let stand for 10 minutes before serving.

Sausage Pizza

Makes 4 to 6 servings.

- 1 15-ounce can tomato sauce
- 1 6-ounce can tomato paste
- 1 clove garlic, crushed
- 1 teaspoon basil
- 1 teaspoon oregano
- 2 12- to 14-inch unbaked crusts
- 1 pound pork sausage, cooked and drained
- 2 cups grated mozzarella cheese
- 1 to 2 onions, sliced
- 1 to 2 green peppers, cut in rings
- ½ pound mushrooms, sliced
- 1 to 2 cans anchovies
- ½ pound pepperoni, sliced
- 1 cup grated Romano or Parmesan cheese

Combine tomato sauce, tomato paste, garlic, basil, and oregano. Spread each crust with half of the sauce. Top with remaining ingredients, ending with Romano or Parmesan cheese. Bake at 450°, in the lower portion of the oven, for 15 to 20 minutes, until crust is brown and pizza is bubbly.

Sausage and Cheese Pie

Makes 6 to 8 servings.

- 1½ pounds bulk pork sausage
- 1 onion, chopped
- 1 9-inch baked pie shell
- 4 eggs, lightly beaten
- ½ cup milk
- 8 ounces Swiss, Cheddar, or sharp American cheese, shredded
- ⅔ cup canned pizza sauce, optional
- 3 slices Cheddar or sharp American cheese, cut in half diagonally, optional

Brown sausage and onion in a large frying pan; drain well. Place in pie shell. Combine eggs and milk; blend thoroughly. Pour over sausage. Spread cheese over top. Bake at 325° for 25 to 30 minutes or until a knife inserted in the center comes out clean. If desired, spread top with pizza sauce and arrange cheese triangles on top. Bake 10 minutes longer, until cheese is melted.

Meatballs Olé

Makes 4 to 6 servings.

- ½ pound ground pork
- ½ pound ground chuck
- 1 slice bread
- ¼ cup milk
- 1 tablespoon vegetable oil
- 2 small onions, chopped
- 1 clove garlic, minced
- 1 6-ounce can tomato paste
- 1 cup beef bouillon
- ¼ cup Burgundy wine, optional
- ½ teaspoon ground cumin
- ½ teaspoon crushed oregano
- 2 teaspoons chili powder
- 1 1-pound can kidney beans, drained

Combine pork, ground chuck, bread, and milk; mix together lightly. Shape into 6 to 8 meatballs. Heat oil in a large frying pan. Brown meatballs on all sides; drain fat. Add onions, garlic, tomato paste, bouillon, wine, and seasonings. Cover and simmer 30 minutes. Add kidney beans. Simmer for 15 minutes. Serve over hot rice.

Manicotti

Makes 3 to 4 servings.

- ½ pound pork sausage
- 1 small onion, chopped
- 1 clove garlic, minced
- 1 tablespoon olive oil
- 1 6-ounce can tomato paste
- 1 16-ounce can Italian plum tomatoes and liquid
- 2 cups water
- ½ teaspoon salt
- ½ bay leaf
- ½ teaspoon basil
- 2 cups shredded mozzarella cheese
- 1 cup ricotta or creamed cottage cheese
- ½ cup grated Parmesan cheese
- 2 eggs, lightly beaten
- ¼ cup snipped parsley
- ½ teaspoon salt
-   Dash black pepper
- 12 manicotti shells

Sauté pork sausage until no longer pink; drain fat. Remove from pan and set aside. Sauté onion and garlic in olive oil until tender. Add pork, tomato paste, tomatoes, water, salt, bay leaf, and basil. Cook over medium heat for 45 minutes to 1 hour, until thick, stirring occasionally. Remove bay leaf. Combine 1 cup of the mozzarella cheese, the ricotta and Parmesan cheeses. Add eggs, parsley, salt, and pepper; mix well. Stuff uncooked manicotti shells with cheese mixture. Spread ½ cup of the sauce in a 9 x 13-inch baking dish. Arrange stuffed manicotti in dish; pour remaining sauce on top. Sprinkle on remaining mozzarella cheese. Cover and bake at 400° for 40 minutes.

Pork Pattie Casserole

Makes 4 to 6 servings.

- 1 pound bulk pork sausage, sliced into 8 patties
- 2 apples, chopped
- 1 onion, chopped
- ¼ cup raisins
- 1 1-pound can sauerkraut, drained
- ½ cup dry white wine
- 2 apples, cored and cut into 8 rings

Brown sausage patties on both sides in a large frying pan. Remove from pan. Drain all but 1 tablespoon fat. Add chopped apples, onion, and raisins. Sauté until onion is tender. Add sauerkraut and wine. Heat for 3 to 4 minutes, stirring often. Place sauerkraut in a shallow baking dish. Arrange pork patties on top. Place an apple slice over each pork pattie. Cover and bake at 350° for 45 minutes.

Meat Burek

Makes 6 to 8 servings.

- 1 pound ground pork
- 1 pound ground beef
- 1 onion, minced
- 1 clove garlic, minced
- ½ teaspoon salt
- ¼ teaspoon black pepper
- ½ teaspoon thyme
- 6 eggs, lightly beaten
- 1 1-pound package phyllo dough, thawed
- ½ cup melted butter

Sauté pork, beef, onion, and garlic until browned; drain fat. Add salt, pepper, and thyme; mix lightly. Remove from heat. Stir in eggs. Place 2 sheets of dough in a greased 9 x 13-inch casserole. Fold edges of dough in to fit pan. Brush with a little of the melted butter. Sprinkle 2 tablespoons of the meat mixture over the dough. Continue layering, using 1 sheet of dough at a time. End with phyllo dough. Fold in edges to fit pan. Brush with remaining melted butter. Score into squares. Bake in a 350° oven for 45 minutes.

Sausage Lasagna

Makes 10 to 12 servings.

1 pound ricotta or cottage cheese
2 eggs, lightly beaten
¼ cup snipped parsley
½ teaspoon salt
1 cup grated Parmesan cheese
¾ pound sliced mozzarella cheese
8 ounces lasagna noodles, cooked

Prepare the Sauce, below. Combine the ricotta cheese, eggs, parsley, salt, and half of the Parmesan cheese; blend thoroughly. Oil a 9 x 13-inch baking dish. Spread ⅓ of the Sauce over the bottom of the dish. Layer half of the noodles and half of the cheese on top. Spread ⅓ of the Sauce over the cheese mixture. Layer remaining noodles and cheese mixture. Top with remaining Sauce. Sprinkle on remaining Parmesan cheese. Arrange sliced mozzarella cheese on top. Bake at 350° for 45 minutes. Let stand for 15 minutes before serving.

Sauce

1 pound hot Italian sausage
1 pound sweet Italian sausage
1 onion, chopped
2 cloves garlic, crushed
1 tablespoon olive oil
1 1-pound can tomatoes
1 8-ounce can tomato sauce
1 6-ounce can tomato paste
½ cup water
½ cup Burgundy wine
1 teaspoon crushed basil
1 teaspoon crushed oregano
½ bay leaf
1 teaspoon salt
1 teaspoon sugar

Remove casing from sausage. Brown in a frying pan; crumble with a fork; drain fat. Set sausage aside. Sauté onion and garlic in oil until tender. Add sausage and remaining ingredients. Simmer for 45 minutes.

Won Ton Soup

Makes 6 servings.

16 Filled Won Tons, recipe below
3 cups chicken broth
1 tablespoon soy sauce
½ teaspoon salt
White pepper to taste
1 scallion, chopped

Prepare Filled Won Tons.

Bring 3 quarts of water to a rapid boil. Carefully add won tons; return to a boil. Boil until won tons float to the surface. (Check to see that won tons are not sticking to the bottom of the pan.) Drain and set aside.

Heat the chicken broth, soy sauce, salt, and pepper. Gently drop cooked won tons into broth. Add scallion. Heat through and serve.

Filled Won Tons

½ pound ground pork
1 tablespoon dry sherry
1 tablespoon soy sauce
1 teaspoon salt, divided
1 cup flour
1 egg

Combine pork, sherry, soy sauce, and ½ teaspoon of the salt in a bowl; mix thoroughly. Set aside while preparing won ton wrappers.

Sift flour and remaining ½ teaspoon salt into a mixing bowl. Break the egg into the flour; blend thoroughly. Turn dough out onto a lightly floured surface. Knead until smooth. Cover dough with a damp towel. Let stand for 20 minutes. Roll dough until paper-thin. Cut into 16 4-inch squares.

Place ½ teaspoon of the pork filling slightly off center of each square. Fold in half diagonally. Moisten edges and press together. Bring the right corner up to the top. Repeat for the left corner. Press lightly to seal.

Saucey Sausage Spaghetti

Makes 4 to 6 servings.

1 pound Italian sausage, casings removed
1 medium onion, chopped
1 clove garlic, crushed
½ pound mushrooms, sliced
1 15-ounce can tomato sauce
¼ cup Burgundy wine
½ teaspoon crushed basil
½ teaspoon crushed oregano
Grated Parmesan cheese

Brown sausage in a large frying pan, breaking it with a fork; drain fat. Add onion, garlic, and mushrooms. Sauté until onion is tender. Add tomato sauce, wine, basil, and oregano. Cover and simmer for 25 minutes. Serve over spaghetti. Sprinkle on Parmesan cheese. (Makes enough sauce for 1 pound spaghetti.)

Lamb Loaf I

Makes 6 servings.

    1 pound ground lamb
      Salt and pepper to taste
  ½ teaspoon dried mint
    1 egg, lightly beaten
  ½ cup soft bread crumbs
    2 tablespoons catsup
    1 teaspoon mustard
    4 tablespoons dry sherry
    1 clove garlic, minced
    1 small carrot, grated
    1 small onion, grated
    3 hard-cooked eggs, shelled

Combine all ingredients, except eggs, in a mixing bowl; mix well. Place half of the lamb mixture in a greased 9 x 5-inch loaf pan. Place the 3 eggs in a row in the center of the loaf. Cover with the remaining lamb mixture. Carefully pack down and smooth top. Bake in a preheated 350° oven for 1 hour. Turn loaf out onto a warm serving platter. Garnish with mint jelly or fruit.

Lamb Loaf II

Makes 6 servings.

    1 pound lean ground lamb
    1 clove garlic, minced
    1 cup cracker or matzo crumbs
    1 cup milk
  ¼ cup minced onion
  ¼ cup minced green pepper
  ¼ cup catsup
    1 teaspoon salt
  ½ teaspoon black pepper

Combine all ingredients in a mixing bowl; blend thoroughly. Place mixture in a lightly oiled 9 x 5-inch loaf pan. Bake at 350° for 45 to 60 minutes or until lamb is no longer pink.

Russian-Style Meat Loaves

Makes 18 mini loaves.

    1 16-ounce loaf frozen white bread dough
  ¾ pound ground beef
    1 onion, chopped
    1 clove garlic, minced
  1½ cups sweet-sour red cabbage, drained
      Snipped green onion
      Sour cream

Thaw frozen bread dough according to package

directions. Sauté beef, onion, and garlic in a large frying pan until meat is browned; drain fat. Stir in cabbage. Divide dough into 18 portions. Roll each piece into a 4-inch circle on a lightly floured board. Place ¼ cup of the meat-cabbage mixture on half of each circle; fold circle in half; seal edges. Place loaves, sealed edge down, on a greased baking sheet. Cover with a towel and let rise about 30 minutes. Bake in a 375° oven for 15 to 20 minutes. Stir green onion into sour cream. Serve with meat loaves.

Sausage-Apple Ring

Makes 8 servings.

    2 pounds bulk pork sausage
  1½ cups dry bread crumbs
    2 eggs, lightly beaten
  ½ cup milk
  ½ small onion, minced
    1 apple, finely diced

Combine pork sausage, bread crumbs, eggs, and milk; blend thoroughly. Stir in onion and apple. Press into a 6-cup ring mold. Bake at 350° for 1 hour or until pork is no longer pink. Drain fat. If desired, fill ring with sautéed apples or scrambled eggs.

Turkey Loaf

Makes 4 to 6 servings.

    2 eggs, lightly beaten
  ¼ cup wheat germ
    2 tablespoons tomato paste
    1 teaspoon salt
  ¼ teaspoon black pepper
    1 pound raw turkey, ground twice
  ¼ pound turkey ham, ground
    2 tablespoons margarine or butter, melted
  ½ cup cranberry sauce, mashed

Combine all ingredients, except margarine and cranberry sauce; mix thoroughly. Place in a greased 8 x 4-inch loaf pan. Bake in a 350° oven for 1 hour and 15 minutes. Brush the top of the loaf with margarine after 30 minutes. Turn out onto an oven-proof platter. Spread top with cranberry sauce. Return to oven for 15 minutes.

Pork Loaf

Makes 8 servings.

  2 slices whole wheat bread, crusts trimmed
½ cup milk
  1 pound ground pork
  1 pound pork sausage
  1 egg, lightly beaten
  1 apple, diced
  1 rib celery, diced
  1 onion, diced
½ green pepper, diced
  1 teaspoon salt
    Pinch nutmeg

Soak bread in milk until milk is absorbed. Combine bread, pork, pork sausage, and egg; mix well. Stir in apple, celery, onion, green pepper, salt, and nutmeg; blend thoroughly. Shape into a loaf in a 9 x 5-inch loaf pan. Bake at 350° for 1½ hours. Serve with baked potatoes and red cabbage.

Reuben Meat Loaf

Makes 8 servings.

  1 15-ounce can tomato sauce with bits
½ teaspoon sugar
  1 pound ground beef
  1 12-ounce can corned beef, chopped
2¼ cups soft bread crumbs
½ onion, minced
  2 eggs, lightly beaten
  1 clove garlic, minced
  1 teaspoon dry mustard
  8 ounces sauerkraut, drained and chopped
½ teaspoon caraway seed, optional
  1 cup shredded Swiss cheese
  2 slices Swiss cheese, cut in 8 triangles

Combine tomato sauce and sugar. Mix together ¼ cup of the tomato sauce, ground beef, corned beef, bread crumbs, onion, eggs, garlic, and mustard. Pat meat firmly into a 12 x 15-inch rectangle on a sheet of waxed paper. Combine sauerkraut, caraway, and shredded cheese. Spread over meat to within 1 inch of edges. Roll up meat, jelly-roll fashion, starting at short edge. Seal seam and ends. Using the waxed paper to lift the roll, gently ease meat loaf, seam-side down, onto a shallow 12 x 8-inch pan. Spread half of the sauce over loaf. Bake at 350° for 60 minutes. Spread remaining sauce over loaf. Bake 10 minutes. Arrange cheese slices over top. Return to oven until cheese melts.

Turkey Pyramid

Makes 4 to 6 servings.

  2 cups ground, cooked turkey or chicken
  1 4-ounce can mushroom stems and pieces, drained
¾ cup leftover turkey gravy or ¾ cup undiluted cream of chicken soup
  2 cups mashed potatoes
¼ cup grated Cheddar cheese
  2 tablespoons butter, melted
¼ cup soft bread crumbs

Combine the first 3 ingredients; blend thoroughly. Shape into a pyramid in a greased, shallow baking dish. Mix potato with half of the cheese. Frost pyramid with potatoes. Drizzle melted butter over top. Combine bread and remaining cheese; sprinkle on top. Bake in a 425° oven for 20 minutes.

Chicken Croquettes

Makes 4 servings.

  1 10¾-ounce can cream of chicken soup
  4 eggs
  2 cups ground or minced chicken or turkey
  1 tablespoon minced onion
  2 tablespoons snipped parsley
  1 teaspoon prepared mustard
¼ cup milk
    Dry bread crumbs
    Peanut oil

Combine cream of chicken soup and 2 of the eggs in a saucepan. Stir in chicken, onion, parsley, and mustard. Bring mixture to a boil, stirring constantly. Pour into a bowl; chill thoroughly. Combine remaining 2 eggs and milk; beat lightly. Shape chicken mixture into 6 balls. Roll balls in bread crumbs to coat completely. Dip into egg-milk mixture, then again in crumbs. Place on a waxed paper-lined platter. Chill for 1 hour. Deep fry croquettes, 2 or 3 at a time, in 365° oil for 5 minutes or until golden brown. Drain on paper toweling. Serve with Mushroom Sauce.

Mushroom Sauce

  1 tablespoon minced onion
  1 tablespoon margarine
  1 10¾-ounce can cream of mushroom soup
¼ cup milk
¼ cup dry sherry

Sauté onion in margarine until golden. Stir in mushroom soup. Gradually stir in milk and sherry. Cook and stir until mixture comes to a boil. Keep hot until serving time.

Pizzaburger Loaf

Makes 6 servings.

- ½ cup chopped onion
- 1 6-ounce can tomato paste
- 1 cup water
- 1 teaspoon salt
- ½ teaspoon black pepper
- 1 teaspoon crushed oregano
- ¼ teaspoon crushed basil
- 1½ pounds ground beef, or combination beef, veal, and pork
- 1 egg, lightly beaten
- 1 cup crushed soda crackers or ¾ cup matzo meal
- 3 ounces mozzarella cheese, thinly sliced and cut in half diagonally

Combine onion, tomato paste, water, and seasonings in a small saucepan. Cover and simmer for 10 minutes or until onion is tender. Remove sauce from heat. In a mixing bowl, combine ground beef, egg, and crushed crackers. Add half of the sauce; blend thoroughly. Shape mixture into a 10 x 6-inch loaf on waxed paper. Carefully place loaf in an 11 x 7-inch baking pan. Bake in a 350° oven for 1 hour. Spoon remaining tomato sauce over top of loaf. Arrange cheese triangles on top. Bake for 10 minutes or until cheese melts.

Roulade

Makes 6 servings.

- 1½ pounds ground beef
- 1 teaspoon salt
- 1 teaspoon minced parsley
- 1 teaspoon dehydrated onion
- 1 egg, lightly beaten
- ½ cup bread crumbs
- ½ teaspoon oregano
- 1 clove garlic, minced
- 8 ounces shredded mozzarella or Cheddar cheese
- 1 15-ounce can tomato sauce and bits
- 2 tablespoons dry Vermouth, optional

Combine all ingredients, except cheese, tomato sauce, and Vermouth, in a mixing bowl; mix lightly. Shape mixture into a 12 x 10-inch rectangle on a sheet of waxed paper. Sprinkle cheese on top to within 1 inch of all sides. Roll up, jelly-roll fashion, pressing ends to seal. Place meat roll, seam-side down, on a shallow pan. Combine tomato sauce and dry Vermouth; blend thoroughly. Spread half of the tomato sauce over the roll. Bake at 350° for 1 hour. Spread remaining sauce over roll; bake 10 minutes.

Stuffed Meat Loaf

Makes 6 to 8 servings.

- 2 pounds ground beef
- 1 teaspoon salt
- 1 egg, lightly beaten
- 3 tablespoons butter or margarine
- 1 cup bread crumbs
- 1 onion, minced
- 1 rib celery, minced
- ½ green pepper, diced
- ½ teaspoon marjoram
- ½ teaspoon thyme
- 3 slices bacon
- 1 10¾-ounce can cream of tomato soup
- ½ cup sour half-and-half
- ¼ cup sherry

Combine beef, salt, and egg in a mixing bowl; mix until egg is thoroughly blended. Divide mixture into 2 equal portions. Pat 1 portion into a 9 x 5-inch loaf pan.

Melt butter in a small frying pan. Add bread crumbs, onion, celery, green pepper, marjoram, and thyme. Sauté until vegetables are just tender. Pat vegetable mixture over meat in pan. Lay bacon strips lengthwise over vegetables. Spoon on remaining meat; smooth top. Combine soup, sour half-and-half, and sherry; blend thoroughly. Spoon half of the sauce over the meat loaf. Bake at 350° for 1 hour. Drain fat. Remove to a warm serving platter. Heat remaining sauce and serve with meat loaf.

Beef-Spinach Loaf

Makes 6 servings.

- 1½ pounds ground beef, or combination beef and veal, beef and pork
- 2 10-ounce packages frozen, chopped spinach, cooked and drained
- 1 medium onion, minced
- 1 cup cooked rice
  Salt and pepper to taste
- 2 large eggs, lightly beaten
- 4 slices bacon

Combine meat and spinach in a large mixing bowl; mix lightly. Add onion, rice, salt, pepper, and eggs; blend thoroughly. Spoon mixture into a lightly oiled 9 x 5-inch loaf pan. Smooth top. Lay bacon strips lengthwise over top. Bake in a 350° oven for 1 hour or until meat is no longer red. Remove to a serving platter.

Basic Crepes

Makes 14 to 16 crepes.

- 1 cup flour
- 1 cup water
- ½ cup milk
- 2 eggs
- 1 tablespoon vegetable oil
- ⅛ teaspoon salt

Combine all ingredients in a blender, food processor, or mixing bowl; beat until batter is very smooth. Cover and refrigerate for at least 2 hours. Heat a lightly greased 6- or 7-inch crepe pan over medium heat until hot. Pour about 2 tablespoonfuls batter into pan, tilting pan quickly to coat bottom. Pour off excess. Cook until lightly browned. Turn out, brown-side up, on tea towels. Repeat until all batter is used. If crepes will not be used immediately, stack on a wire rack with waxed paper separating crepes. Cover to prevent drying out. Wrap in freezer wrap or foil; freeze. To thaw, remove outer wrap and let stand at room temperature until thawed.

Stacked Veal Stroganoff Crepes

Makes 6 servings.

- 12 crepes
- 2 tablespoons vegetable oil
- 1 small onion, chopped
- 1½ pounds ground veal
- 2 tablespoons flour
- 1 cup beef bouillon or broth
- 2 tablespoons tomato paste
- 1 teaspoon salt
- ¼ teaspoon black pepper
- 1 tablespoon Worcestershire sauce
- 1 4½-ounce can mushroom stems and pieces, drained
- ¼ cup red wine
- 1 cup sour cream

Heat oil in a large frying pan. Brown meat and onion; drain fat. Stir in flour. Cook for 2 minutes. Add bouillon, tomato paste, salt, pepper, Worcestershire sauce, and mushrooms; mix lightly. Stir over moderate heat until thickened and bubbly. Stir in wine and sour cream. Heat through; but do not boil. Layer crepes in a shallow pan spooning some of the meat mixture between crepes. Continue layering, ending with meat sauce. Heat in a 350° oven for 5 to 7 minutes. Slice into pie-shaped wedges.

Broccoli-Ham Crepes

Makes 4 servings.

- 8 crepes
- 1 10-ounce package frozen, chopped broccoli, cooked and drained
- 1 10¾-ounce can cream of mushroom soup
- 1 cup ground, cooked ham
- 1 tablespoon dry sherry
- ½ cup sour cream at room temperature

Combine hot broccoli with cream of mushroom soup, ham, and sherry; mix well. Divide the broccoli-ham mixture among the crepes; roll each up. Arrange crepes on a warm serving platter. Pour sour cream down the center of the crepes.

Manicotti Crepes

Makes 6 to 8 servings.

- 12 crepes
- 2 tablespoons butter or margarine
- 1 small onion, chopped
- 1 clove garlic, minced
- ¾ pound ground beef
- 1 10-ounce package frozen, chopped spinach, cooked, drained and squeezed dry
- ½ teaspoon salt
- ⅛ teaspoon black pepper
- ¼ cup grated Parmesan cheese
- 8 ounces mozzarella cheese cut into 12 thin slices

Heat butter in a large frying pan. Add onion and garlic; sauté until golden. Add beef. Stir and cook until brown; drain fat. Stir in spinach, salt, pepper, and Parmesan cheese. Divide mixture among crepes; roll up loosely. Place crepes in a lightly greased, shallow baking pan. Top each crepe with a cheese slice. Spoon sauce over cheese. Bake at 350° for 20 minutes or until bubbly.

Sauce

- 4 tablespoons butter
- 4 tablespoons flour
- 2¼ cups milk
- 2 tablespoons dry sherry
- ½ teaspoon salt
- ⅛ teaspoon black pepper
- ¼ cup grated Parmesan cheese

Melt butter in a heavy saucepan. Blend in flour; cook for 2 minutes, stirring constantly. Gradually stir in milk. Cook and stir until sauce thickens and comes to a boil. Stir in sherry, salt, pepper, and cheese. Cook until cheese is melted.

Florentine Cups

Makes 4 to 6 servings.

12 crepes

Butter the outside of each crepe. Fit each crepe into a muffin tin, buttered-side down. Divide Filling among crepes. Bake at 350° for 40 minutes or until eggs are set.

Filling

- ½ pound ground lamb
- 1 clove garlic, crushed
- 1 small onion, chopped
- ½ teaspoon salt
- 8 to 10 mushrooms, sliced
- 1 10-ounce package chopped spinach, thawed, drained, and squeezed dry
- 3 eggs, lightly beaten
- ½ cup milk

Sauté lamb, garlic, onion, salt, and mushrooms until meat is no longer pink. Stir in spinach; simmer 2 to 3 minutes. Drain thoroughly. Add meat mixture to eggs and milk.

Turkey Crepes

Makes 6 to 8 servings.

- 18 to 20 5-inch crepes
- 2 tablespoons butter
- 1 tablespoon vegetable oil
- 3 tablespoons chopped onion
- 2 cups sliced mushrooms
- 2 cups chopped, cooked turkey
- 1 cup Sauce, below
- ¼ cup grated Parmesan or Swiss cheese

Heat butter and oil in a small saucepan. Add onion and mushrooms; sauté until just tender. Remove from heat. Add turkey and just enough Sauce to hold mixture together. Place 1½ tablespoons of the turkey mixture in the center of each crepe; roll up. Place in a buttered baking dish. Spoon remaining Sauce over top. Sprinkle on cheese. Bake 10 to 15 minutes at 350°. Place under broiler for 1 or 2 minutes to brown the top.

Sauce

- 1 10¾-ounce can cream of celery soup
- ½ cup sour half-and-half
- 1 tablespoon sherry

Combine all ingredients in a small bowl; blend thoroughly.

Ham and Cheese Crepes

Makes 6 to 8 servings.

- 12 crepes
- 2 tablespoons butter or margarine
- 1 medium onion, minced
- 1 cup ground, cooked ham
- 1 large tomato, peeled, seeded, and chopped
- ½ teaspoon crushed basil
- ¼ teaspoon black pepper
- 2 tablespoons snipped parsley
- 4 ounces Swiss cheese, shredded
- ¼ cup butter or margarine, melted
- ½ cup grated Parmesan cheese

Heat butter in a saucepan. Add onion and sauté until soft. Stir in ham, tomato, basil, and pepper. Cook until almost dry, stirring constantly. Remove from heat. Stir in parsley. Place 1 tablespoon of the filling and 1 tablespoon of the Swiss cheese on the edge of each crepe; roll up. Place, seam-side down, in a lightly greased 9 x 13-inch baking dish. (Crepes can be covered and refrigerated for several hours, if desired.) Brush tops with melted butter and sprinkle on Parmesan cheese. Broil 4 inches from heat until lightly browned.

When browning hamburger, try using a bulb baster to remove grease from the pan.

Canneloni Crepes

Makes 5 to 6 servings.

- 16 crepes
- 1 pound cooked chicken, minced
- 2 10-ounce packages frozen, chopped spinach, cooked and drained
  Salt and pepper to taste
  Dash nutmeg
- 1 egg, lightly beaten
- 1 cup heavy cream
- 4 tablespoons brandy
- ½ cup grated Parmesan cheese
  Paprika

Combine chicken, spinach, salt, pepper, nutmeg, egg, ¼ cup of the cream, and brandy; blend thoroughly. Place 2 tablespoons of the mixture on each crepe; roll up. Arrange crepes in a lightly buttered, shallow baking dish. Pour remaining cream on top. Sprinkle on cheese and paprika. Bake at 350° for 40 minutes or until lightly browned.

Index

E
F
G
H
I
K
L
M